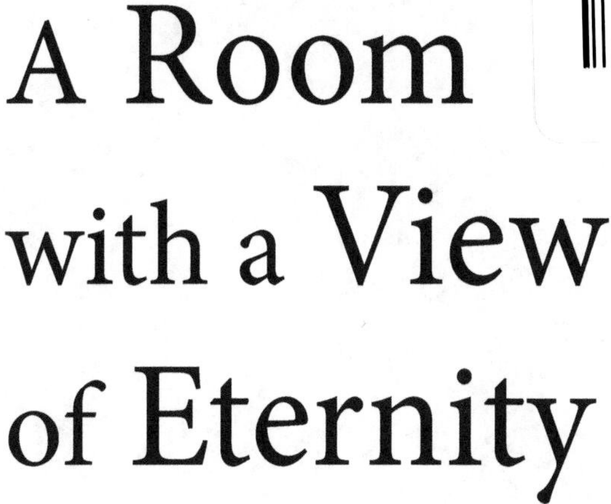

A Room with a View of Eternity

The Last Will & Testament of the Lord Jesus Christ

John 13-17

Shari S. Abbott

To those who have inherited the promised gifts.

. . .rejoice, because your names are written in heaven.
Luke 10:20

These things have I written unto you
that believe on the name of the Son of God;
that you may know that you have eternal life, and
that you may believe on the name of the Son of God.
1 John 5:13

A Room with a View of Eternity

The Last Will & Testament of the Lord Jesus Christ

That I may publish with the voice of thanksgiving,
and tell of all thy wondrous works. (Psalm 26:7)

Published by Psalm267 Publishing
www.psalm267.com

All emphasis and bracketed information added.

Printed in the United States of America

ISBN: 978-1-7361076-6-9

Table of Contents

A Room with a View of Eternity

Psalm267 Publishing

That I may publish with the voice of thanksgiving, and tell of all thy wondrous works. (Psalm 26:7)

Jesus
SPOKE
I AM THE LIGHT
OF THE WORLD
he who follows me
SHALL NOT WALK IN
DARKNESS
but shall have the
LIGHT of LIFE
JOHN 8:12

. . . a large upper room furnished . . .

and they made ready the passover.

And when the hour was come, he sat down,

and the twelve apostles with him.

Luke 22:12, 13-14

Introduction

A Room with a View of Eternity

THIS BOOK INVITES YOU TO TAKE A SEAT AT THE LORD'S TABLE. Spend time with Jesus during His final hours on earth, and hear Him speak words of comfort, love, and promise to His disciples.

We'll do this by entering into the upper room, which is described for us by the apostle John in chapters 13-17 of his gospel account.

The first 12 chapters of John's Gospel tell of Jesus' public ministry. Chapter 13 begins the historical account of the events that took place on the night in which Jesus was betrayed. In these chapters, we read of a private and intimate discourse between Jesus and His 12 disciples as they shared a Passover meal in the upper room of the home of a friend. During and after the meal, Jesus prepared His disciples for what was to come. He began by washing their feet (chapter

Leviticus 23:1-4 And the LORD spoke unto Moses, saying, Speak unto the children of Israel, and say unto them, Concerning the feasts of the LORD, which ye shall proclaim to be holy convocations, even these are my feasts. Six days shall work be done: but the seventh day is the sabbath of rest, an holy convocation; ye shall do no work therein: it is the sabbath of the LORD in all your dwellings. These are the feasts of the LORD, even holy convocations, which ye shall proclaim in their seasons.

Collectively these three convocations are called the Feasts of the Lord. They were to be observed annually—Passover in the spring, Shavuot in the early summer, and Tabernacles in the fall. These feasts are also referred to as the appointed times, the feast days, the Festivals of the Lord, and the Pilgrim Feasts.

Observing these feasts was required under Levitical law and specific instructions were given about how to observe them, including where to observe them. God commanded His people to make a pilgrimage to Jerusalem at each of the three appointed times (Exodus 23:17, 34:23, Deuteronomy 16:16) to observe the feasts in His holy city.

The Time of Passover for Jesus and His Disciples

Jesus gathered with His disciples in the evening of the first day of the week-long Passover celebration. This day was Nisan 14. It was called the Day of Preparation (Leviticus 23:5) and it was a day of sacred assembly.

Leviticus 23:7 In the first day ye shall have an holy convocation: ye shall do no servile work therein.

On the first day of the week of Passover, Jesus and His disciples shared a Passover meal. However, it must be noted, that this was not the Feast of the Passover, which is called the Feast of Unleavened Bread. That feast took place on the second day of Passover, on Nisan 15 (Leviticus 23:6). It was at that meal that the Passover lamb was eaten.

The meal that Jesus and His disciples shared took place during the evening hours of Nisan 14. We must remember that a Jewish day was different than our day. A Jewish day began in the evening hours, after sundown. It progressed to the morning and afternoon hours, and ended at sunset the following evening. It did not begin as our day does—at midnight. Therefore, when Jesus and the disciples gathered during the evening hours of the Day of Preparation, the lamb for the Passover meal had not yet been killed. The lambs would be killed during the daytime hours that followed the nighttime hours.

Verses That Cause Confusion

There are several verses in which Jesus spoke of eating the Passover with His disciples (Matthew 26:17, Mark 14:14, Luke 22:18, 15, et al.). When Jesus said "Passover," He was not referring to the Feast of the Passover, also known as the Feast of Unleavened Bread. The confusion is cleared up by understanding that the word "Passover" has been used, and still is used, in three different ways by God's people and in biblical accounts. "Passover" can mean: 1) The week-long festival (also called the days of unleavened bread); 2) The actual Feast of the Passover on Nisan 15 (also called the Feast of Unleavened Bread); or 3) The lamb that was sacrificed and eaten at the Feast of Unleavened Bread.

When Jesus said, "With desire I have desired to eat this passover with you before I suffer" (Luke 22:15), He was making reference to the evening meal on the Day of Preparation (Nisan 14) being a passover meal. He was not referring to the actual Feast of the Passover (Nisan 15), or to the Passover lamb, which had not yet been sacrificed.

We know this from John's Gospel:

> *John 13:1 Now before the Feast of the Passover [the Feast would be at least 24 hours later on Nisan 15], when Jesus knew that his hour was come that he should depart out of this world unto the Father [His departure would be during the daylight hours of the Day of Preparation, Nisan 14], having loved his own which were in the world, he loved them unto the end.*

> *John 13:2a And supper being ended [this supper was simply a meal during Passover that He shared with His disciples]...*

A Misconception About the Meal

There is nothing to suggest that this was a Jewish Seder as many think it was.

The Jewish Seder is a tradition of the Jews. It is not one of the Feasts of the Lord found in the book of Leviticus. The Feasts of the Lord were prescribed by the Lord and commanded to be observed. The Jewish Seder is a ritualistic meal with customs that were added over time. It became so highly ritualized that it was given the name "Seder," which is a word meaning "order."

According to jewishvirtuallibrary.com, the Seder meal is to take place on "the first night of Passover (the first two nights outside of Israel)." Jews around the world "are commanded to have a special family meal filled with ritual to remind [them] of the significance of the holiday."

The celebration of the Seder was first prescribed in the Haggadah. Haggadah means "telling," however, it should be understood that the Haggadah is not the telling of the words of the Lord. It is the telling of Jewish traditions.

The Seder meal is a Jewish tradition and, although it remembers God's deliverance of the nation of Israel from Egyptian bondage, the rituals performed are not found in God's instructions for the remembrance of Passover. Leviticus 23 clearly states God's directives regarding how His people were to commemorate the first Passover, and how they were to celebrate the Feast of Unleavened Bread as a memorial of His delivering them out of bondage.

We should not confuse Jesus' Last Supper with a Jewish Seder. Nor should we confuse it with the Feast of Unleavened Bread. The supper Jesus shared with His disciples was a fellowship meal on the first day of Passover, therefore, the Bible refers to it as a Passover meal (Luke 22:15). This would be similar to having a Christmas party on any day in December other than Christmas day.

A Passover Meal of Great Significance

At this Passover meal, Jesus prepared His disciples for what was about to happen. This would be His last meal with them (more information on the Last Supper can be found in the appendix). With the breaking of bread and the offering of the cup of wine, Jesus prophetically and symbolically proclaimed His imminent death on the cross. However, the disciples did not understand that the bread represented His body that would soon be broken, and the wine represented His blood that would soon be shed.

They did not understand that Jesus would be killed the next day at the same time the Passover lambs would be slaughtered. Jesus would be the perfect and final Passover Lamb, as prophesied by John the Baptist:

> *John 1:29 ...Behold the Lamb of God, which taketh away the sin of the world.*

Jesus, the Lamb of God, would atone for the sins of the world by His shed blood (Isaiah 52:13-53:12). He would be the Deliverer whom God had promised in the Garden (Genesis 3:15) and the One who would conquer death and open the way for man to be fully restored to God (John 3:16).

Unlike the animal sacrifices in the Temple, Jesus' blood would do more than just cover their sins. Jesus' blood would remove their sins (Psalm 103:12) by washing their sins away (Revelation 1:5).

Not only did the disciples not understand the prophetic words of Jesus, John, and the prophets, they also did not comprehend how their lives were soon to change. They had been called by Jesus to follow Him in the three and a half years of His earthly ministry, but soon He would be gone. Then they would learn to follow Him as the Risen Lord. And everything would change.

Take A Seat at the Master's Table

> *Luke 4:4 Jesus answered him, saying, It is written, That man shall not live by bread alone, but by every word of God.*

Let's now join the disciples at the Master's table and partake of the same spiritual food that Jesus gave them—His words—words of truth, hope, and love. As we "sit at the table," we'll be "with Jesus" during His final hours of human life. We will "hear" His words, spoken to His disciples (John 13-16), and His most beautiful prayer, spoken to His Father (John 17). We'll "hear" Jesus bequeath the glorious gifts that are His alone to give. These gifts are more than we could ever hope for, and far more precious than we can ever imagine.

Now, let's spend a few hours in the presence of the Master, in. . .

A Room with a View of Eternity.

The Spirit of the Lord

is upon me, because he hath anointed me to **preach** the gospel to the poor; he hath sent me to **heal** the broken-hearted, to **preach** deliverance to the captives, and recovering of sight to the blind, to **set at liberty** them that are bruised, to **preach** the acceptable **Year of the Lord.**

Luke 4:18-19

Chapter 1

Love Beyond Measure

John 13

Chapters 13-17 in the book of John beautifully present a picture of the God-Man who came not to be served but to serve (Mark 10:45), and to seek and save the lost (Luke 19:10).

Jesus revealed His mission early in His ministry, when He went into the synagogue, asked for the scroll of the prophet Isaiah, opened it, and read the words. Isaiah prophesied of the Spirit coming upon the Messiah, of God anointing the Messiah to preach, and of God sending Him to bind up the broken-hearted, to proclaim liberty to the captives, to open the prison, to proclaim the acceptable year of the Lord (Isaiah 61:1-2a), and the day of vengeance of our God; to comfort all that mourn.

When Jesus read Isaiah's words in the Temple (Luke 4:18-19, 21), He stopped after reading, "to proclaim the acceptable year of the Lord (Isaiah 61:2a). Jesus omitted "and the day of vengeance of our God; to comfort all that mourn." Why did Jesus omit the warning of God's vengeance?

The answer is revealing. In Jesus' first advent, He had come to do all the things Isaiah had prophesied, except proclaiming "the Day of Vengeance of the Lord." Jesus came to bring light into a dark world and salvation to mankind. He came to live a sinless human life, to prepare God's people to receive their Messiah, to go to the cross to pay for the sins of the world, and then to rise again defeating sin and death. In Jesus' earthly ministry, His works made Him known, His words inspired hope, and His redemptive work opened the way for man to be restored to God. Therefore, Jesus proclaimed His first advent to be "the acceptable year of the Lord" and said, "This day is this scripture fulfilled in your ears." (Luke 4:19, 21)

Two Days

1. "This day" — the day in which the acceptable year of the Lord was fulfilled.

2. "The day" — the day of vengeance of our God.

These are two very different days. Although separated by only a comma in the text of Isaiah, they are separated by more than 2,000 years in the reality of time. "The acceptable year" was Jesus' first advent. "The day of vengeance" will be Jesus' second advent when He will return to judge the earth and all its inhabitants. However, even in that judgment, Jesus will have mercy upon those who turn to Him in faith. He will "...comfort all that mourn" (Isa 61:2).

Holy Ground

John 13-17 is filled with the Lord's words of love, hope, and amazing blessings. This section of Scripture is often referred to as holy ground because it so beautifully reveals Jesus' amazing and unending love, His sacrificial service, and His precious promises. These chapters also tell of the great revelation Jesus gave to His disciples — to give hope and assurance to them who heard these words spoken and to all people who will read these words throughout the centuries.

In the Upper Room, Jesus began to prepare His disciples by speaking plainly to them, He revealed His impending sacrificial death—something they did not want. He also told them of the great gifts they would receive after His death—something they did not expect. But most importantly, He told them of His abiding love for them—something they did not comprehend.

"He loved them unto the end. . ."

> *John 13:1 Now before the feast of the passover, when Jesus knew that his hour was come that he should depart out of this world unto the Father, having loved his own which were in the world, he loved them unto the end.*

In the upper room of the house of a friend, on the Day of Preparation (Nisan 14), Jesus' heart and His thoughts were focused on those whom He loved. Jesus had come in love, "For God so loved the world that He gave His only begotten Son" (John 3:16) and Jesus would depart in love, "He loved them unto the end." The "end" speaks of both the end of His public ministry and the end of His earthly life. And the "end" would take place in less than 24 hours.

While loving them "unto the end" has a temporal sense, the Greek language conveys a much deeper meaning. The

Greek word for "end" is "telos," which means "to the fullest" or "to the uttermost." Therefore, this magnifies Jesus' love as being a full and steadfast love, a love without end, an undying, unfailing, unbounded love, that is eternally lavished on His own through His unrelenting grace.

In the upper room, Jesus showed His love when He served His disciples, ministered to their troubled hearts, promised them hope, and gave them a glimpse into the glorious union He has with the Father—a union they would soon have with Him.

Jesus' Last Supper

Jesus sat down for this Passover meal, during the evening of Nisan 14, knowing that it would be His last supper, and, more so, the last time he would be with His disciples before His death.

It is critically important to understand how a Jewish day began and ended during the appointed times (the Feasts of the Lord). It is often said that a Jewish day commenced at sundown (or sunset) and continued until the next sundown, but that is not true for the Lord's appointed times—the Sabbaths and the Holy Days.

Nightfall versus Sundown

Sundown, or sunset (Hebrew: shkiah), is defined as the moment the trailing edge of the sun's disc disappears below the horizon to the west. Nightfall (Hebrew: tzeit hakochavim) occurs when three stars are visible in the sky.

The time from sundown/sunset to nightfall is a period of twilight. Twilight is the time when the sun has set below the horizon, but there remains refraction and scattering of the sun's rays into the atmosphere. Twilight is a period of half-light or semi-darkness. It's a period of diminishing light that progresses toward complete darkness (nightfall). Twilight is considered a time period of ambiguity because the Jews could count the twilight period in the current day or they could count it in the coming day. . .with the exception of Sabbath Days and Holy Days.

- Sabbath and Holy Days began at sunset, which is the earliest possible sign of night when the disc of the sun disappears below the horizon.
- Sabbath and Holy Days lasted through the daytime hours until nightfall (the sighting of three stars in the night sky).
- Sabbath and Holy Days included the twilight period at both the beginning of the day and at the end of the day.

These days, appointed by the Lord, included all hours of light—full, partial, and even diminishing light.

On the Day of Preparation, during the nighttime hours (which began at sunset and included the twilight hours), Jesus and his disciples ate a meal and then walked to the Garden of Gethsemane. We all know what happened next. Jesus prayed in the Garden and was then betrayed by Judas and arrested in the dark of night. Again, remember that the nighttime hours of a Jewish day preceded the daytime hours. These things took place during the nighttime hours of Nisan 14 and during the daytime hours that followed Jesus was crucified — a the very hour that the Passover lambs were being slaughtered. This fulfilled the words of Isaiah, "He was led as a lamb to the slaughter. . ." (Isaiah 53:7).

Jesus Washed Their Feet

Mark 10:45 tells that Jesus came "not to be ministered unto [to be served], but to minister [serve]. . ." and in washing the feet of His disciples, He did just that.

Foot washing was the work of the lowliest of servants. In those days, people walked long distances, on very dusty roads, wearing sandals. Their feet got very dusty and dirty. Therefore, it was customary for the host of a meal to arrange for a servant to wash the guests' feet prior to the meal.

While the disciples would have gladly washed Jesus' feet, they would never have washed one another's feet. Peers did not do this. Peers did not consider themselves to be servants of one another. Only for a master—for a person of a higher authority—would one humble himself to perform a servant's task. Therefore, it would have surprised the disciples when Jesus put the servant's towel around His waist, filled a basin with water, and began to wash their feet (John 13:4-5).

Before or After the Meal?

The King James and New King James Bibles tell us that the foot washing took place after the meal ended (John 13:2). However, foot washing was always done before eating. So was it before or after?

Both the KJV and NKJV translate the Greek word "ginomai" in John 13:2 as "being ended." Other Bibles translate it as "during supper" (RSV, NASB, et.al.) and as "the evening meal was being served" (NIV). Strong's Dictionary defines that word as "to cause to be," "to become (come into being)," "to arise," "be brought to pass," "be performed," etc. But Strong's also tells that it can be translated as "be done," "be ended," and "be finished." So how do we know which translation is correct? Two sources give an answer.

1. The Greek word is "ginomai." It is a genitive singular masculine, aorist middle participle, and therefore indicates the foot washing took place when the meal began.

2. The Scripture clearly defines the time of the foot washing. Luke 22:20 tells that after the meal was ended, Jesus offered the cup of wine and revealed that one of the 12 would betray Him.

Luke 22:20-21 Likewise also the cup after supper, saying, This cup is the new testament in my blood, which is shed for you. But, behold, the hand of him that betrayeth me is with me on the table.

And Matthew tells that after the cup was offered, they left the Upper Room and went out into the mount of Olives.

Matthew 26:28, 30 For this is my blood of the new testament, which is shed for many for the remission of sins... And when they had sung an hymn, they went out into the mount of Olives.

Since the meal ended, the cup was offered, and then they departed the upper room, it's clear that the best translation of "ginomai" is "during supper" and that the foot washing took place as the meal was beginning, which was a Jewish custom for sanitary reasons.

Judas Still Present

When the foot washing took place, the devil had already put into the heart of Judas to betray Jesus (John 13:2). And yet, Jesus washed the feet of all twelve of His disciples — including Judas.

Jesus moved from one disciple to the next as He washed their feet. When He came to Peter and knelt down to wash his feet, Peter questioned, ". . .Lord, dost thou wash my feet?" (John 13:6). Peter knew that Jesus was His Lord and he did not feel worthy to have His Master wash his feet. Peter did not understand the significance of what Jesus was doing, and the following conversation ensued:

John 13:7-8 . . .What I [Jesus] do thou knowest not now; but thou shalt know hereafter. Peter saith unto him, Thou shalt never wash my feet. Jesus answered him, If I wash thee not, thou hast no part with me.

No part with Him! Heaven forbid. That was the last thing Peter would have wanted to hear. He loved Jesus and was devoted to Him. Peter's desire was to be with Jesus. To have no part with Jesus was unthinkable, and so Peter responded, with unbridled love. . .

> *John 13:9 Lord, not my feet only, but also my hands and my head.*

Peter wanted all that Jesus had to give him. With his response he was saying, wash every part of me so that I might have more of You. Peter was saying,

- Cleanse my mind, so that my thoughts may be pure.
- Cleanse my heart, so that I might show Your love.
- Cleanse my hands, so that they might serve You.
- Cleanse my feet, so that I might go where You lead me.

Peter did not understand the cleansing about which Jesus was speaking. So Jesus continued to teach. . .

> *John 13:10 (NKJV) Jesus said to him, "He who is bathed [washed] needs only to wash his feet, but is completely clean; and you are clean..."*

These words reveal a beautiful picture of being washed in the blood of Christ. Once we are "washed. . .in His own blood" (Revelation 1:5) we are cleansed (1 John 1:7). We are justified—made completely clean. Our sins are washed away, our souls are regenerated by His Spirit, and we receive the Lord's righteousness credited to us. Yet, our feet still need to be washed—again, and again, and again.

John the Baptist illustrated this teaching in a prophetic picture. John came preaching a gospel of repentance and water baptism for the remission of sins. John the Baptist fully washed those who came to him. The person was fully immersed in the Jordan River, but the river water could never fully wash away their sins. John came to prepare the way for Jesus, who would wash sinners in His blood. Jesus would give more than remission of sins, He would give complete redemption from sins—a redemption purchased at a great price (Acts 20:28). He would give a complete cleansing of the stain of sin—a cleaning that would make them "white as snow" (Isaiah 1:18). And He would regenerate their souls—a regeneration of washing and renewing by the Holy Spirit (Titus 3:5).

Only the blood of the Lamb of God can cleanse a sinner of every sin ever committed and every sin they ever will commit. Only the blood of Jesus can fully wash us and make us completely clean (Revelation 1:5). And only the gift of the Holy Spirit can keep, teach, and guide us in the paths of righteousness.

Dirty Feet

As Christians, the blood of Jesus has washed away all our sins, so why do our feet still need washing? It is because our feet "anchor" us to this world. Once a repentant sinner is saved, he is spiritually united with Jesus and his new citizenship is in Heaven (Philippians 3:20). However, those who belong to Jesus and remain on this earth are pilgrims here (Hebrews 11:13, 1 Peter 2:11), walking an earthly path that leads to the heavenly home Jesus has promised.

Our shoes serve as a separation between us and the world, just as did the sandals of God's ancient people. You might remember how God instructed Moses to remove his sandals when he stood on holy ground. God was removing that separation. Symbolically, our shoes represent a form of protection from the dirt of the world and a covering that protects our feet so we can go forth with "the preparation of the gospel of peace" (Ephesians 6:15).

Sojourning on earth, we continue to sin and our feet still get dirty. There is no way to avoid this. But we don't need to take a full bath, because we've already been washed by the blood of Jesus (Revelation 1:5). All we need is to have our "feet washed" by Jesus and He does that by the "washing of water by the word."

> *Ephesians 5:25-27 . . .as Christ also loved the church [those who belong to Jesus], and gave himself for it; That he might sanctify and cleanse it [believers] with the washing of water by the word, That he might present it to himself a glorious church, not having spot, or wrinkle, or any such thing; but that it should be holy and without blemish.*

Our sins can never destroy or diminish our son-ship as a child of God, but our sins will affect our fellowship with God. Therefore when we sin, we must be quick to return to Jesus and confess our sins. When we do so, He is faithful and just to forgive us our sins, and to cleanse us from all unrighteousness. (1 John 1:9)

Love One Another

When washing the disciples' feet, Jesus knew that:
1) Judas would soon betray him,
2) Peter would soon deny him, and
3) The disciples would soon scatter.

Yet, Jesus loved them and washed the feet of all 12 disciples. Contrast that with Pilate who, after he had sent Jesus to His death, took a basin of water and attempted to wash his hands of the matter. Love will always use the "basin" Jesus filled with "water by the Word," not the "basin" Pilate filled with power-less water that can never wash away sin.

Loving Friends and Enemies

Just as Jesus came to serve (Mark 10:45) and took on the "form of a servant. . .and humbled Himself" (Philippians 2:7-8), we are to do the same. Jesus often spoke to His disciples of the importance of loving service. In the upper room He said to them:

> *John 13:14-17 If I then, your Lord and Master, have washed your feet; you also ought to wash one another's feet. For I have given you an example, that you should do as I have done to you. Verily, verily, I say unto you, The servant is not greater than his lord; neither he that is sent greater than he that sent him. If you know these things, happy are you if you do them.*

Consider what Jesus might have felt as he washed the feet of Judas and looked up into his eyes. And what might Judas have felt, knowing what he had agreed to do? He had already covenanted with the chief priests and elders to deliver Jesus into their hands (Matthew 26:15) and the devil had already put into Judas's heart to betray Jesus (John 13:2). Jesus knew this, as indicated by His words to Peter:

> *John 13:10 . . .<u>you</u>* [Peter] *<u>are clean, but not all of you</u>* [a reference to Judas].

At this time, Judas had already received the thirty pieces of silver from the chief priests and elders as payment to turn Jesus over to them.

It's interesting to note that this was the price of redemption paid for a slave (Exodus 21:32), but now it was the price of betrayal of the Master.

The Betrayer Revealed

With the washing of the disciples' feet completed, Jesus took his place at the table with them. He sat down and continued to teach. As Jesus spoke, He revealed that one of them would betray Him. Jesus then told His disciples that He knew who it would be..

John 13:18 I speak not of you all: I know whom I have chosen: but that the scripture may be fulfilled, He that eateth bread with me hath lifted up his heel against me.

The Gospel of Matthew records this very clearly and tells of the confusion the disciples had when the Lord said, ". . .one of you shall betray me.."

Matthew 26:22 And they were exceeding sorrowful, and began every one of them to say unto him, Lord, is it I?

Desiring to know who would do such a thing, Peter prompted John to ask of the Lord.

John 13:23-25 Now there was leaning on Jesus' bosom one of his disciples, whom Jesus loved. Simon Peter therefore beckoned to him, that he should ask who it should be of whom he spoke. He then lying on Jesus' breast saith unto him, Lord, who is it?

At this time Judas' heart had already turned and been hardened and Jesus did something to reveal him as the betrayer:

John 13:26 He it is, to whom I shall give a sop [a piece of bread], when I have dipped it. And when he had dipped the sop, he gave it to Judas Iscariot, the son of Simon.

John 13:27-28, 30 And after the sop Satan entered into him [Judas]. Then said Jesus unto him, That thou doest, do quickly. Now no man at the table knew for what intent he spoke this unto him. . .He [Judas] then having received the sop went immediately out: and it was night.

Betrayed by a Friend Whom He Loved

Have you ever been betrayed by a friend or a family member? Betrayed by someone you love beyond measure and thought you could fully trust? Betrayal by those who are closest to us, those whom we care for deeply and love most dearly, is very painful. It is different than the attacks or rejections from acquaintances or adversaries.

- Betrayal by a loved one can feel like death. And in many ways, it is a death. While it's not physical death, betrayal can lead to a relational death.
- Betrayal is always a form of disloyalty to the relationship, occurring when love diminishes and selfish desires increase.
- Betrayal breaks the bond of trust and, more often than not, brings an end to fellowship.
- Betrayal cuts more deeply than rejection or opposition, and, in many cases, it is toxic to the point of despair or depression.
- Betrayal can only come from those who are close—a close friend or a family member.

The closer the friend or family member, the greater the pain of betrayal. Singer/songwriter Michael Card, in his song, "Why," addressed this:

> Only a friend can betray a friend,
> A stranger has nothing to gain.
> And only a friend comes close enough,
> To ever cause so much pain.

Betrayal is one of the most painful experiences and if it has happened to you, take heart. It happened to Jesus also.

Jesus had chosen Judas to be one of His twelve disciples. The disciples had left everything to follow Jesus, and that included Judas. For three and a half years, Judas had been a part of Jesus' circle of closest friends. He had been taught by Jesus. He had been a part of Jesus' ministry work. And he had fellowshipped with Jesus and the other disciples daily.

Judas was fully loved by Jesus, but in those final days of Jesus' ministry and life, Judas revealed the deceit and wickedness of his heart. His heart was cold, hard, and without love. Had Judas's heart been that way from the beginning? Or did his heart wander and he then joined himself to those who sought to destroy Jesus?

Why Judas betrayed Jesus, we do not know because the Bible doesn't say. But we can understand the pain Jesus must have felt. Jesus sat at dinner that evening knowing that His friend would soon betray Him—and knowing that he would do so with a kiss, a gesture of affection becoming a means of betrayal.

For those of us who have experienced betrayal by someone we love, there is comfort in knowing that Jesus understands our pain. He understands because He experienced it when Judas kissed Him (Matthew 26:21) and, to a much lesser extent, by the actions of the other 11 disciples. Peter denied Jesus three times (Luke 22:34) and all the disciples fell away and scattered (Matthew 26:31). But the faithful returned.

Faithful Love

While man is capable of such betrayal, Jesus is not. He gives us a faithful love that is forever steadfast and eternally secure. He is the only One in whom we can fully trust. . .

> *For He Himself has said [promised], "I will never leave you nor forsake you." (Hebrews 13:5)*

In the Greek, the word "never" in Hebrews 13:5 is a triple-negative. It can be translated, never, never, absolutely never. That's an assurance of Jesus' loyal love, the light that shines in our darkest hours, the tender touch that comforts in our deepest despair, and the faithful promise that gives certain hope in all things.

As painful as betrayal is, we can find purpose in knowing that we are, in some way, and to some extent, sharing in the fellowship of Jesus' sufferings. As Paul desired, we also should desire to "know him, and the power of his resurrection, and the fellowship of his sufferings, being made conformable unto his death." (Philippians3:10)

Pastor and evangelist, F. B. Meyer (1847-1929, a contemporary of D. L. Moody), said: "For whom the heart of man shuts out; the heart of God shuts in."

When Judas's heart shut Jesus out, Jesus found His comfort in the heart of His Father. Just as we share in the fellowship of Jesus' sufferings, and might be shut out by the heart of a betrayer, we also find our comfort and peace in trusting the heart of God. We might not understand the circumstances that surround us, but we can know that our God is in control and we can call to mind the words of an old, but forever true, saying of encouragement: When we can't trace God's hand, We can always trust His heart.

Jesus lived in perfect submission to His Father's purpose and plan, knowing that His Father is Sovereign over all things. Our comfort and rest are also found in trusting God's sovereign plan for each of us.

Scottish pastor, author, and poet, George MacDonald, penned these words in 1864 in his poem titled, *Rest.* These words both inspire trust and offer rest in our great God.

The wind of words may toss my heart,
But what is that to me!
'Tis but a surface storm—Thou art
My deep, still resting sea.

The Faithful Remain

With Judas's departure (John 13:30), Jesus was left alone with His 11 faithful disciples. He began to speak openly and plainly to them. His first words were an announcement of His and the Father's glory. He said, "Now is the Son of man glorified…" (John 13:31)

It's interesting to note that once Judas left, Jesus said, "NOW is the Son of man glorified. . ." Judas had gone to make arrangements about the manner in which he would betray Jesus, and, with this action, the Lord's journey to the cross began.

Consider that Jesus spoke saying that He was NOW glorified. At this moment, in Jesus' perspective, all was finished. Jesus knew that everything would come to pass in exact accordance with His Father's plan. Therefore, Jesus was at that time glorified, having done His Father's will since His incarnation and now completing His Father's plan in what was certain to unfold very soon.

> *"Now is the Son of man glorified, and God is glorified in him." (John 13:31)*

In making this proclamation, Jesus used the Messianic title "Son of Man." This was the title Daniel the prophet used when, in a vision, he saw the Son of Man going before the Ancient of Days and being given everlasting dominion, and glory, and a kingdom that shall never be destroyed. (Daniel 7:13-14)

The Messianic title, Son of Man, is found 84 times in the Gospels of Matthew, Mark, Luke, and John. In all but one use, this title is used by Jesus in speaking of Himself. The exception is found in the account of the Sunday morning events when the two angels in the tomb used this title when speaking of Jesus. However, even in that case, the angels were quoting Jesus' words.

> *Luke 24:6-7 He is not here, but is risen: remember how he spake unto you when he was yet in Galilee, Saying, The Son of man must be delivered into the hands of sinful men, and be crucified, and the third day rise again.*

When Jesus said, "Now is the Son of man glorified, and God is glorified in him" (John 13:31), He knew that the atonement for sin would soon be made. But as the disciples heard his words, they would have understood the Son of Man as meaning the promised Messiah, the anointed one who would be King. They still did not understand that His death was certain and that, in dying, He would conquer death, and Satan would be vanquished.

As Jesus continued to teach the 11 faithful disciples, He called them "little children." This is a term of endearment, and it reminds us that those who belong to Jesus are children of God. It also reminds us that, as God's children, we are dependent upon Him to love and care for us. This endearment was remembered well by the apostle John, for he used it nine times in his first epistle.

Addressing the 11 in this way, Jesus told them that He would soon be leaving them and they could not come with Him. Then He gave them a new commandment:

> *A new commandment I give unto you, That ye love one another; as I have loved you, that ye also love one another. By this shall all men know that ye are my disciples, if ye have love one to another. (John 13:34-35)*

Jesus was clear about the importance of loving one another. During His earthly ministry, Jesus had given two commandments about love: 1) Love God and 2) Love your neighbor as yourself. New He elevates our command to love. Rather than loving your neighbor as yourself, we are to love like Jesus love us!!! That is pure, true, steadfast, sacrificial love.

Love unites us together as His Body and loving others demonstrates that we are His. Jesus commanded this three times. Here in John 13 and twice in John 15.

> *This is my commandment, That ye love one another, as I have loved you. (John 15:12)*

> *These things I command you, that ye love one another. (John 15:17)*

Love is, therefore, the most important part of our identity and our testimony. Because God is love (1 John 4:8, 16), when we love and serve others, we reflect His love.

Wandering, Forgetting, and Falling

Chapter 13 draws to a close with Peter vowing his allegiance to the Lord. It's clear that Peter truly loved the Lord, but we also know that Peter was weak. A short time after his declaration of love and allegiance, Peter denied Jesus. Peter's need for self-protection, eclipsed his love for Jesus. His denial took place after a slow drift in the wrong direction.

First, his heart had wandered. As evidenced by his boastful declaration, "Though all shall be offended, yet will not I" (Mark 14:29). His declaration should have been: Though all shall be offended, Lord, help me never be.

Next, Peter fell asleep (Mark 14:37). Jesus had told him to be watchful and pray, but Peter failed to remember the Lord's command.

Then Peter began to fall. He followed "afar off" (Matthew 26:58), and seated himself at the fire in the presence of the Lord's enemies (Mark 14:54, Luke 22:56). Finally, just as Jesus had prophesied, Peter denied knowing Jesus (Luke 22:60).

Peter's wandering, forgetting, and falling is a good reminder to us of the necessity to be diligent in guarding our hearts (Proverbs 4:23). This is our most important stewardship, to keep our hearts devoted to the Lord, to establish our hearts in His grace, and to love our God with our heart, soul, mind, and strength. From that will flow a steadfast love.

May Peter be an example to us of the importance of being devoted to Jesus. May we always remember the importance of following near Jesus and not drifting away, of being obedient to His commands to be watchful and pray, and of not becoming self-assured but always being dependent on Him.

Soul Care for the Betrayed

The Psalmist tells us that "those who sow in tears shall reap in joy." (Psalm 126:5) Take comfort and find joy in knowing that Jesus is present in your troubles. Find rest in the peace that only He can offer, "knowing that from the Lord you will receive the reward of the inheritance; for you serve the Lord Christ" (Colossians 3:24). This poem, from an unknown author, sums it up so beautifully:

Whatever your cross, whatever your pain,
There will always be sunshine, after the rain.

Perhaps you may stumble, perhaps even fall;
But God's always ready, to answer your call.

He knows every heartache, He sees every tear,
A word from His lips, can calm every fear.

Your sorrows may linger, throughout the night,
But suddenly vanish, by dawn's early light.

The Saviour is waiting, somewhere above,
To give you His grace, and send you His love.

—Author unknown

Chapter 13 of John ends with the eleven faithful disciples having troubled hearts. Jesus had told them things they did not want to hear. He told them things that were confusing and unsettling. Their confusion was growing and their hearts were burdened. Therefore, Jesus spoke again and gave them blessed assurance of the comfort and rest that only He can give.

Jesus did not tell them to stop being troubled. He understood their emotions and He acknowledged their troubled hearts. He knew that these emotions would increase in the days ahead when He would be crucified and then gone from them. Therefore, Jesus proceeded to give His disciples answers and reasons that would provide them with the comfort, peace, and rest that they would so desperately need.

As we move into chapter14, we find recorded the Lord's words of hope—true hope—that only He can give.

A NEW COMMANDMENT I GIVE YOU:
LOVE ONE ANOTHER
AS I HAVE LOVED YOU
SO YOU MUST **LOVE ONE ANOTHER**
BY THIS EVERYONE WILL KNOW
THAT YOU ARE MY DISCIPLES,
IF YOU **LOVE ONE ANOTHER**

John 13:34-35

JESUS
ANSWERED,
"I AM THE WAY
THE TRUTH AND
THE LIFE.
NO ONE
COMES TO
THE
FATHER
EXCEPT
THROUGH
ME."
JOHN 14:6

Chapter 2

A Promised Home

John 14

With the departure of Judas (John 13:30), Jesus began to speak openly to His faithful 11 disciples. The Lord's words, beginning in John 13:31 and ending with John 17, are often referred to as the "Upper Room Discourse," "The Lord's Final Discourse," or "The Lord's Farewell Message."

Jesus would soon be leaving His disciples, so, in the same way, others before Him had done (Moses in Deuteronomy 31-33, Joshua in Joshua 23-24), Jesus prepared His followers.

The disciples had not fully understood Jesus' act of service when He washed their feet. Nor had they fully understood what He had told them. They were both confused and troubled.

After having told them that He was going away and that they could not accompany Him (John 13:33), Peter inquired of Jesus, asking where He would be going, and Jesus answered, "Where I am going you cannot follow Me now, but you shall follow Me afterward" (John 13:36). This did not answer Peter's question. And, it appears that Jesus' words caused great concern.

Chapter 14 of John opens with Jesus comforting the 11, telling them they have nothing to fear, and that they should not worry about anything. His words were emphatically directed to Peter, and to all the disciples, to settle their minds and comfort their hearts.

> *John 14:1 Let not your heart be troubled: you believe in God, believe also in me.*

> *John 14:2-3 In my Father's house are many mansions: if it were not so, I would have told you. I go to prepare a place for you. And if I go and prepare a place for you, I will come again, and receive you unto myself.*

When Jesus concluded by telling them "where I go you know, and the way you know" (John 14:4), their lack of understanding was evidenced by Thomas. Thomas spoke up and said that they did not know where Jesus was going, and then asked how they could know the way. Jesus' response was clear and forthright. He spoke the sixth of the seven "I am" statements recorded in the book of John. In doing so, Jesus proclaimed Himself to be the only way to the heavenly home in His Father's house and the only way to the Father Himself.

> *John 14:6 Jesus saith unto him, I am the way, the truth, and the life: no man cometh unto the Father, but by me.*

John 14:1-6 present both a revelation of how to enter into Heaven and a precious promise of eternal life with Jesus. This passage is often used at funerals and memorial services.

It is Not Death to Die

I chose the John 14 passage to eulogize my dear friend Jacky, who went to be with Jesus in December 2011. Throughout her battle with pancreatic cancer, Jacky knew where she would go if God did not heal her. Jacky knew "the way"—more specifically, Jacky knew the Person who is "the way." Her trust in Jesus and her confidence in His promise of Heaven gave her strength beyond her physical ability. This was most beautifully exhibited in her final days.

The day before her death, my husband and I sat with Jacky. As I held her hand and looked into her blue eyes, she was so very weak and barely able to speak. Yet her eyes conveyed the blessed assurance that she had in Jesus. There was an unmistakable brightness, a restful peace, and a sparkle of life and hope in her eyes. She seemed to speak to me with her eyes and I believe she was "saying" that she knew what awaited her, she knew the way, and she knew her Saviour was waiting to welcome her home.

Throughout Jacky's 18 month battle with cancer, she was a picture of the untroubled heart of John 14:1. She experienced difficult times and physical challenges, yet she remained strong in her faith and at peace throughout her treatments. In our women's Bible study we would gather around her every week and pray for her healing. She loved the prayers offered by her sisters-in-Christ, and she told us that she could literally feel our prayers and they gave her peace.

Our prayers were not answered in the way we had hoped. But God was gracious and blessed Jacky with 18 months of life, much more than she had anticipated when she was first diagnosed.

As Jacky journeyed "through the valley of the shadow of death," her faith was unshakable and her confidence was steadfast. She knew and trusted that Jesus would deliver her from cancer. Whether it would be on this earth or in Heaven, she knew that she would be healed (Romans 8:28, John 14:3). In the face of her most troubling times, she had the promised peace that only Jesus can give:

> *John 14:27 Peace I leave with you, my peace I give unto you: not as the world giveth, give I unto you. Let not your heart be troubled, neither let it be afraid.*

God healed Jacky completely when He received her to Himself, and she entered into the heavenly home prepared for her. Jacky's dying was a strong witness of God's gifts of strength and peace and it was a beautiful testimony of her faith in Jesus. It was Jesus who strengthened and comforted Jacky with the peace of God that passes all understanding (Philippians 4:7), the peace that give both confidence and hope.

It's no surprise that Jacky's favorite verse was one that so many cherish. It's a verse that many turn to for assurance in difficult times:

> *Romans 8:28 And we know that all things work together for good to them that love God, to them who are the called according to his purpose.*

Not everyone can embrace that verse when they are suffering. But Jacky understood the words because she understood the sovereignty of God, the grace of God, and His unfailing love in the worst of times. She had lost her husband years before in a boating accident. She knew how it felt to have your heart broken and your life shattered—to be left a widow at a young age with a young child. She also knew what it was to receive comfort and strength from God to carry on in the face of such severe grief, the pain of loss, and her future of widowhood and single parenting.

Jacky knew that God is sovereign and that He was working His perfect plan and His perfect purpose in her life—even when it hurt so much. Jacky faced her battles in life with faith, trusting that the Lord would bring her through it, and knowing that He was working all things together, for His glory and her good.

Six years later another dear friend, Tad, was diagnosed with pancreatic cancer. The doctors were unable to perform the surgery that could offer hope for survival, and 19 months later, he went to be with the Lord. However, during those 19 months, he continued to live fully by the grace of God. He taught a weekly Bible study almost to the end, and he seized every opportunity to be a testimony to the goodness, grace, and faithfulness of Jesus. By his confidence, peace, and joy in the face of physical suffering and approaching death, and with his proclamation of the gospel, many of his lost friends came to know Jesus, and others who had wandered from Jesus drew closer and grew in their desire to know Him better.

My husband and I have some wonderful memories of our last time with Tad. Standing by his bedside, the day before he died, Tad was ready to go home to Heaven and he was filled with joy. We talked about faith and hope, God and Heaven, Scripture, and more. Although his body was dying, his mind was very much alive and he recalled Scripture verses and passages with amazing accuracy and clarity. At one point, I said, "Just think, Tad, soon you'll see Jesus." With a smile, he replied, "I can hardly wait." Tad was a longtime Bible study teacher, so I added, "When Steve and I join you in Heaven, we want you to have a Bible study. And we want you to get Paul to teach it!" In typical Tad style, with confidence and excitement, he immediately responded, "I can do that!"

Both of these friends are a reminder that when our time comes to leave this earth, our dying can be a faithful testimony to the presence and goodness of God in our lives and the hope of glory that He offers to all who belong to Jesus.

While we remain on this earth, we are called to share our

faith with confidence in the Lord's words of promise, peace, and assurance of our final resting place in Heaven.

John 14:3 I will come again, and receive you unto myself; that where I am, there ye may be also.

May we always remember that Jesus awaits our arrival with open arms to receive us into His presence. He prayed for this in His final hours with His disciples.

John 17:24 Father, I will that they also, whom thou hast given me, be with me where I am.

Our eternal life and unity with Jesus began when we received Him as our Lord and Saviour. But there is an even greater unity yet to come when we enter into our heavenly home.

Unity Revealed in the Upper Room

As the evening meal continued in the upper room, Jesus began to reveal to the disciples the mystery of His union with His Father. He also told them that He would be going to His Father.

John 14:11 Believe me that I am in the Father, and the Father in me. . .

John 14:12 Verily, verily, I say unto you, He that believeth on me, the works that I do shall he do also; and greater works than these shall he do; because I go unto my Father.

The disciples knew that Jesus was speaking of their God — the God of Israel and the God of their fathers, Abraham, Isaac, and Jacob. However, they were still unable to comprehend the full meaning of Jesus' words. Their understanding would be opened sometime later—after Jesus' death, burial, and resurrection; and after they received further instruction, revelation, and the gift of the Holy Spirit.

Knowing they would one day recall and understand His words, Jesus continued to teach His disciples. He told them of the power of His name and that through Him they could ask anything of God.

> *John 14:13-14 And whatsoever ye shall ask in my name, that will I do, that the Father may be glorified in the Son. If ye shall ask any thing in my name, I will do it.*

Asking in Jesus' Name

It's common for Christians to close their prayers with the words, "in Jesus' name." The biblical authority for doing so comes from the verses you just read (John 14:13-14).

There is nothing magical about closing a prayer "in Jesus' name." While this is not a requirement, it should be understood that these three words do have significance.

"In Jesus' name" is an acknowledgment and a reminder of the power of the Name above all names (Philippians 2:9) and the authority in His Person. Jesus told the disciples they could "ask anything in [His] name." This should be understood to mean "according to His power and authority." In other words, "with God, all things are possible" (Matthew 19:26, Mark 10:27, Luke 18:27).

Jesus is God and it is because of His finished work on the cross and His victory over sin and death that the way to the Father has been opened to us. It is by the salvation we have in Him, and by calling on His name (Romans 10:13), that we can come boldly before the throne of grace with our petitions (Hebrews 4:16). That's why we pray in Jesus' name!

The Name Above All Names

The name of Jesus is to be revered and exalted above all

names. It is "at the name of Jesus every knee shall bow" and "confess that Jesus is Lord" (Philippians 2:10-11). "Jesus" is the beautiful name of the One "whom having not seen we love," and having not seen "we believe and rejoice with joy unspeakable and full of glory" (1 Peter 1:8).

Obedience to the One We Love

In verse 15 we encounter a change of subject. After having spoken to His disciples about their troubled hearts, and providing them with an assurance of peace and the comfort of hope, the Lord challenged them to demonstrate their love for Him.

John 14:15 If ye love me, keep my commandments.

During His earthly ministry, Jesus clearly taught that His commandments are to ". . .love the Lord thy God with all thy heart, and with all thy soul, and with all thy mind," (Matthew 22:37) and to ". . .love thy neighbor as thyself." (Matthew 22:39) When we remember who Jesus is, and what He has done for us, our minds are filled with an understanding of His amazing love. His love both humbles us and fuels us to respond in love and gratitude, and with a desire to serve and obey His commandments.

In the book of Ecclesiastes, we find another exhortation to keep the commandments of the Lord. After 11 chapters that speak of the futility of seeking purpose, meaning, joy, and satisfaction "under the sun" (in worldly things), the final chapter closes with. . .

Ecclesiastes 12:13 Let us hear the conclusion of the whole matter: Fear God, and keep his commandments: for this is the whole duty of man.

The keeping of God's commandments is the "conclusion of the whole matter" and "the whole duty of man." That certainly signifies the importance of living in accordance with God's will. It's interesting to note that the word "duty" in Ecclesiastes 12:13 is not found in the Hebrew text. The word is italicized in our Bibles, which indicates that it was added to the English translations. Reading the verse without the word reveals an even greater sense of our purpose in life.

> "...*Fear God and keep His commandments: for this is the whole of man.*"

The "whole of man" is to "fear God and keep His commandments." It's no wonder Jesus said to His disciples, "If ye love me, keep my commandments" (John 14:15). Borrowing from the Westminster Shorter Catechism, our purpose in life is to "glorify God and enjoy Him forever." Living according to God's will and ways bring glory to God.

There is futility in seeking purpose and meaning in anything other than God. We know that worldly things, those things "under the sun," will never satisfy. Knowing Jesus and loving Him generates satisfaction, contentment, and internal peace, which produces abounding joy in the Lord and out-flowing love and service for our neighbors. By this, we are known as His disciples (John 13:35).

Jesus' Departure

The thought of Jesus leaving them must have been very disturbing. The disciples had given up everything, leaving behind their families, their jobs, and their possessions, to follow Him. Jesus had comforted them with hope, by telling of His return for them (John 14:3), and now He promised to send them a Comforter—One who would not only be with them but would also be in them.

> *John 14:16-18 And I will pray the Father, and he shall give you another Comforter, that he may abide with you*

for ever; Even the Spirit of truth; whom the world cannot receive, because it seeth him not, neither knoweth him: but ye know him; for he dwelleth with you, and shall be in you. I will not leave you comfortless: I will come to you.

In these verses, we see a clear revelation of the Triune God. Jesus the Son spoke and told them that they would be comforted by "Another Comforter, the Holy Spirit, who would be sent by God the Father. Jesus assured the disciples that they would know the Comforter and explained how the Comforter would dwell with them. Then Jesus made the statement, ". . .I will come to you."

While these words were reassuring, the disciples could not have fully understood what Jesus meant. As Jews, they did not understand the triune nature and being of God. As Jews, they had been taught that God was one (Deuteronomy 6:4). When Jesus told them that He is One with the Spirit and that God is His Father, it would have been confusing for them. They could not have understood the three distinct Persons of the One Triune God, nor could they have comprehended the unity of the Father, Son, and Spirit.

For more than three years, they had listened as Jesus spoke in parables and gave explanations of what He taught, but now Jesus spoke plainly to them, yet they still could not understand. . .

"I go unto my Father" (verse 12). *". . .the Father. . .shall give you another Comforter. . ."* (verse 16). *". . .you know Him; for He dwells with you . . ."* (verse 17). *". . .I will come to you"* (verse 18).

Jesus spoke of His departure and then said they would see Him. It's no surprise that the disciples were confused.

John 14:19 Yet a little while, and the world seeth me no more; but ye see me: because I live, ye shall live also.

Stand Strong in the Lord

As Jesus continued to speak to His disciples, He spoke of the first of many gifts that He would give to them. He promised His peace (John 14:27) and He told them that He had revealed these things so they would be ready and able to stand strong in adversity.

John 14:27, 29 Peace I leave with you, my peace I give unto you: not as the world giveth, give I unto you. Let not your heart be troubled, neither let it be afraid. And now I have told you before it comes to pass, that, when it is come to pass, ye might believe.

Just as Jesus prepared His disciples for difficult times to come, Jesus also prepares all of us for trials and tribulation. As we depend on Him, we receive strength from Him. In the most difficult times, in the Valley of Weeping, He takes us from strength to strength (Psalm 84).

The Lord has promised to be with us and to never leave or forsake us (Hebrews 13:5).

He is an ever-present help in all things (Psalm 46:1) and His Word encourages, empowers, and motivates us to stand strong in Him.

Romans 14:4 . . .for God is able to make him stand.

1 Corinthians 2:5 That your faith should not stand in the wisdom of men, but in the power of God.

1 Corinthians 16:13 Watch ye, stand fast in the faith. . . be strong.

2 Corinthians 1:24 . . .for by faith ye stand.

Galatians5:1 Stand fast therefore in the liberty wherewith Christ hath made us free. . .

Ephesians 6:11 Put on the whole armour of God, that ye may be able to stand against the wiles of the devil.

Philippians 4:1 Therefore, my brethren. . . stand fast in the Lord, my dearly beloved.

1 Thessalonians 3:8 For now we live, if ye stand fast in the Lord.

2 Thessalonians 2:15 . . .stand fast, and hold the traditions which ye have been taught. . .

One of the best verses of assurance of the power we have to stand strong in Christ is a verse in Colossians. Paul speaks of the "riches of glory" and the presence of Christ in believers.

Colossians 1:27 To whom God would make known what is the riches of the glory of this mystery among the Gentiles; <u>which is Christ in you</u>, the hope of glory.

This presence of Christ "in you" (a Christian), is exactly what Jesus shared with the disciples when He spoke of sending the Comforter, the Holy Spirit. We eagerly anticipate a heavenly paradise and going to be with Jesus, but while we remain on earth Jesus is here with us.

When Jesus saved us, He gave us His Holy Spirit, and that is the mystery of which Paul wrote, "Christ in you, the hope of glory." Note that verse does not say Christ with you. It also does not say, Christ and you. It says Christ IN you! Never forget, and never take for granted, the power of the indwelling Holy Spirit. He is the power of the resurrection. He is the third person of the Trinity. And He is God. He dwells in us and guides us. He teaches and strengthens us. And He enables and empowers us to stand strong in Christ. . .our hope of glory.

It is not death to die,
To leave this weary road,
And 'midst the brotherhood on high
To be at home with God.

It is not death to close
The eye long dimmed by tears,
And wake in glorious repose
To spend eternal years.

It is not death to bear
The wrench that sets us free
From dungeon chain, to breathe the air
Of boundless liberty.

It is not death to fling
Aside this sinful dust,
And rise, on strong, exulting wing,
To live among the just.

Jesus, Thou Prince of life!
Thy chosen cannot die:
Like Thee, they conquer in the strife,
To reign with Thee on high.

Lyrics by César Malan (1832)

I AM the vine
YOU ARE THE BRANCHES
HE THAT ABIDES IN ME
& I IN HIM
THE SAME BRINGS FORTH MUCH FRUIT
For without me YOU CAN DO NOTHING
John 15:5

Chapter 3
The True Vine
John 15

The book of John records seven statements made by Jesus about Himself. Each statement starts with the Lord's claim, "I am."

1) John 6:35, 2—I am the bread of life.
2) John 8:12, 9:5—I am the light of the world.
3) John 10:7, 9—I am the door of the sheep.
4) John 10:11, 14—I am the good shepherd.
5) John 11:25—I am the resurrection and the life.
6) John 14:6—I am the way, the truth, and the life.
7) John 15:1, 5—I am the true vine.

In this chapter, we find Jesus' seventh "I am" statement.

Jesus had just given His disciples a theological explanation of His unity with the Father and His unity with them (John 14:10-11). He also assured them that, "At that day ye shall know that I am in my Father, and ye in me, and I in you" (John 14:20). Then He gave them a horticultural example of this unity with His seventh and final "I am" statement. Jesus told His disciples, "I am the true vine" (John 15:1, 5).

The True Vine

Israel was an agrarian culture, so Jesus' example of the vine would have been very relevant to the disciples. It would have been easily understood.

The abundance of fruit in the region dates back prior to Israel's entering the land. Numbers 13 tells of Moses being instructed by God to send men into the Promised Land to determine the conditions of the land as well as the strength or weakness of the people dwelling there.

> *Numbers 13:18-20 . . .the land, what it is; and the people that dwelleth therein, whether they be strong or weak, few or many; And what the land is that they dwell in, whether it be good or bad; and what cities they be that they dwell in, whether in tents, or in strong holds; And what the land is, whether it be fat or lean, whether there be wood therein, or not. And be of good courage, and bring of the fruit of the land. Now the time was the time of the firstripe grapes.*

The Fruit of the Vine

According to Guinness World Records, the largest bunch of grapes was grown in Chile in1984. It weighed 20 pounds, 11.5 ounces. Hampton Court Palace in England boasts the largest grapevine in the world measuring more than 12 feet in circumference with branches about 108 feet long. Nearly 250 years old, this one vine produces about 600 pounds of grapes per year!

Such an abundance of grapes is what the men, sent by Moses, found at the Brook of Eshcol in the Promised Land. They returned bearing a cluster of grapes so large that it took two men to carry it upon a pole.

Numbers 13:23-24 Then they came to the Valley of Eshcol, and there cut down a branch with one cluster of grapes; they carried it between two of them on a pole. They also brought some of the pomegranates and figs. The place was called the Valley of Eshcol, because of the cluster which the men of Israel cut down there.

This cluster of grapes was a foretaste of God's promise of abundance that awaited the nation of Israel in the land. It represented God's pledge to them of their full inheritance. It remains today a symbol for the nation. Two men carrying a staff laden with a large cluster of giant grapes is the symbol for Israel's Ministry of Tourism.

Known as "The Grapes of Eshcol," the image represents the bountiful harvest in the "land of milk and honey" (Exodus 3:8, et al.) and the prosperity and sweetness of life in the land that God had promised to Israel.

There are many references to the fruitful vine and many mentions of grapes throughout the Bible. Vineyards and the fruit of the vine are referred to in more passages than any other plant in the Bible. References include grapes, grape juice (new wine), fermented grape juice (wine), and raisins.

We can trace grapes all the way back to the first mention in the Bible when Noah planted a vineyard after the flood (Genesis 9:20). And many Bible scholars think that the forbidden fruit in the garden was a grape. This seems plausible, because of the typology of wine and blood. God proclaimed that "the life is in the blood" and it is "blood that makes an atonement for the soul" (Leviticus 17:11). And during this meal in the upper room, Jesus proclaimed that wine represented His shed blood (Mat 26:28, Mark 14:24, Luke 22:20).

Perhaps the fruit of the vine goes all the way back to the Garden. However, we do not know. But we do know that grapes were a very significant crop for the nation of Israel.

The Fall Harvest

We also know from the Bible that grapes in Israel were harvested in the fall at the time of the fruit harvest, the time of the Feast of Tabernacles. The fruit of the vine was an important part of Israel's diet and economy, and the vine and its fruit even served as a prophetic and typological symbol of the nation in numerous Scripture passages, including,

> *Psalm 80:8 You have brought a vine [the people of Israel] out of Egypt...*

> *Isaiah 5:7 For the vineyard of the LORD of hosts is the house of Israel*

> *Jeremiah 2:21 Yet I had planted thee a noble vine, wholly a right seed. . .*

It is certainly understandable why Jesus used a vine in His teaching and associated the grapevine with Himself. Jesus was the Promised Seed from the beginning (Genesis 3:15). He came from the nation of chosen people, called out by God through Abraham, Isaac, and Jacob. Remember that Jacob's name was changed by God to Israel, and it was through his 12 sons that the nation was born. Then, in the fullness of time, God sent Jesus, born of a woman from the tribe of

Judah, the House of Israel. Jesus was the fulfillment of the Promised Seed and He was and is the True Vine. Eternal life came through His blood.

Although Israel was called "a vine" by David and the prophets, the nation was often a fruitless vine. In John 15:1, Jesus called Himself the True Vine and His Father, "the husbandman" (vine-dresser).

Jesus taught that branches (representing believers) would come forth from the True Vine—and some branches would bear fruit and others would be fruitless (John 15:2-6). He also taught that the key to bearing fruit is abiding.

Abiding in the Vine

When Jesus told His disciples of the unity between Himself and His Father (John 14:11, 20), He was speaking of a union of love that flows between them. With the example of the True Vine, Jesus spoke of the riches of the union that the disciples would have in Him. He told them this unity would be a living union through which His love would flow into them and by which they would grow and produce fruit.

Jesus spoke of the importance of abiding (remaining and enduring) in that union. Four times Jesus exhorted his disciples to abide. He also warned them of the dangers of not abiding.

> *John 15:4-5 Abide in me, and I in you. As the branch cannot bear fruit of itself, except it abide in the vine; no more can ye, except ye abide in me. I am the vine, ye are the branches: He that abideth in me, and I in him, the same bringeth forth much fruit: for without me ye can do nothing.*

> *John 15:6 If a man abide not in me, he is cast forth as a branch, and is withered; and men gather them, and cast them into the fire, and they are burned.*

A branch cannot bear fruit apart from the vine (John 15:4). In fact, Jesus told them, ". . .for without me ye can do nothing" (John 15:5). This must be understood to mean that without Jesus man can do nothing in service to the Lord, for we know that even non-believers are capable of doing many things. However, even in their best works, non-believers do nothing of significance in God's eyes, because their works are not done to glorify God. Their strength and power to do good works comes from themselves, not from abiding in the True Vine and the Lord working in and through them.

Jesus made it clear that the purpose of our good works is to glorify God:

> *John 15:8 Herein is my Father glorified, that ye bear much fruit. . .*

Rooted and Built Up in Jesus

In their agrarian culture, the Jews would have clearly understood the importance of the branch abiding in the vine. Paul spoke in a similar manner, using an agricultural example and taught that as Christians we are rooted and grounded in the True Vine!

> *Ephesians 3:17, 19 That Christ may dwell in your hearts by faith; that ye, being rooted and grounded in love. . . might be filled with all the fullness of God.*

> *Colossians 2:7 Rooted and built up in him, and established in the faith, as ye have been taught, abounding therein with thanksgiving.*

Let no one tell you that we, as Christians, are rooted in Israel. We are rooted and built up in Jesus, the seed of Israel, the True Vine.

Jesus revealed to His disciples that this unity, of which He was speaking, would be theirs when He was glorified. Once again, the disciples would not have understood His words. Their understanding would come only after the Lord's resurrection and glorification and His sending of the Holy Spirit.

> *Ephesians 1:17-18 That the God of our Lord Jesus Christ, the Father of glory, may give unto you the spirit of wisdom and revelation in the knowledge of him: The eyes of your understanding being enlightened. . .*

Although the disciples did not yet have the Holy Spirit to open their understanding, the parable of the True Vine helped them in understanding what was to come. They knew that a branch, detached from the vine, would wither and die. They knew that a branch needs the vine to provide sustenance to grow. In just a short time, Jesus would give to His disciples all that they would need to grow in love for Him, in living for Him, and in abiding and resting in Him.

Just as the branches need the vine to live and to grow, the vine needs the branches to bear fruit. While this parable in no way minimizes God's omnipotence and all-sufficiency in Himself, it does teach the importance of our role in God's purpose and plan. It is God's desire to use us, His people, to spread His message of redemption throughout the world and to produce the fruit of righteousness and service.

Jesus is the True Vine and we are His branches. What a privilege we are given, to be partakers in the True Vine and to be participants in what God is doing here on earth.

Although the disciples understood the necessity for a branch to remain attached to the vine to produce fruit, they could not fully understand the unity of which Jesus spoke. The spiritual union and the sustenance of the Holy Spirit remained mysteries to them. But the day would come when they would receive the Holy Spirit and He would help them recall and understand Jesus' words. The Lord would also raise-up another, the apostle Paul, who would teach this lesson in greater depth and help them to better understand what it means to abide in the True Vine.

The Gift of Holy Communion

Matthew, Mark, and Luke tell that at this meal in the upper room, Jesus gave the disciples bread and wine and proclaimed them to be symbolic of His body and blood.

> *Matthew 26:26-28 And as they were eating, Jesus took bread, and blessed it, and brake it, and gave it to the disciples, and said, Take, eat; this is my body. And he took the cup, and gave thanks, and gave it to them, saying, Drink ye all of it; For this is My blood of the new covenant, which is shed for many for the remission of sins.*

> *Mark 14:22-24 And as they did eat, .Jesus took bread, and blessed, and brake it, and gave to them, and said, Take, eat: this is my body. And he took the cup, and when he had given thanks, he gave it to them: and they all drank of it. And he said unto them, This is my blood of the new testament, which is shed for many.*

> *Luke 22:19-20 And he took bread, and gave thanks, and brake it, and gave unto them, saying, This is my body which is given for you: this do in remembrance of me. Likewise also the cup after supper, saying, This cup is the new testament in my blood, which is shed for you.*

How appropriate that Jesus had spoken of Himself as being the True Vine and then told His disciples that the juice that flows from the fruit of the grapevine would take on a new significance for them. It would serve to remind them of His blood, shed for mankind's sin. By partaking of the fruit of the vine in this manner, they would remember Him and His redeeming work. By remembering they would more fully abide in the True Vine.

Do This In Remembrance

As a practice of remembrance, communion is similar to the twelve stones erected as a memorial to God's deliverance of Israel into the Promised Land (Joshua 4). That memorial was set up so the people of future generations would remember what the Lord had done for them.

The memorial of bread and wine was given by Jesus to His disciples—and for all who would come to Him—to be a reminder of Jesus' deliverance of mankind from the bondage to sin and the penalty of sin. Partaking of communion reminds us that Jesus died for us, His body was broken and His blood was shed, opening the way to eternal life in Him.

Communion is also referred to as The Lord's Supper or The Lord's Table. All of these are fine ways to describe the breaking of bread and the cup of wine, but calling it "Holy Communion" reminds us that it is set apart from the world—and it is only for those who belong to the Lord Jesus Christ. The bread and wine are not intended for non-believers and should never be offered to them or taken by them. It is for those who are redeemed by Jesus, purchased by His blood, forgiven of their sins, and given new life in Him.

Paul wrote Jesus' words about communion in his letter to the Corinthian church:

> *1 Corinthians 11:24-25 And when he had given thanks, he brake it, and said, Take, eat: this is my body, which is broken for you: this do in remembrance of me. After the same manner also he took the cup, when he had supped, saying, This cup is the new testament in my blood: this do ye, as oft as ye drink it, in remembrance of me.*

Paul added an exhortation to partake often to remember the Lord's death:

> *1 Corinthians 11:26 For as often as ye eat this bread, and drink this cup, ye do show the Lord's death till he come.*

These things
I have spoken unto YOU
that IN ME YOU
might have PEACE
in the world
you shall have TRIBULATION
but be OF GOOD CHEER
I HAVE OVERCOME
The World
John 16:33

Chapter 4

In A Little While

John 16

Jesus spoke these things hoping to encourage and strengthen His disciples for what was to come. Jesus was preparing them to stand strong in the face of affliction and adversity, for the time of His departure was fast approaching.

John 16:5-6 But now I go my way to him that sent me; and none of you asketh me, Whither goest thou? But because I have said these things unto you, sorrow hath filled your heart.

The Comforter

Understanding their sorrow, Jesus explained to them that He must go away so He could send the Comforter.

John 16:7 Nevertheless I tell you the truth; It is expedient for you that I go away: for if I go not away, the Comforter will not come unto you; but if I depart, I will send him unto you.

"Comforter" is such a beautiful name for the third person of the Trinity. It reminds us that we are assured of the Lord's presence and of His peace in our lives. The name "Comforter" is both who the Spirit is and what He does.

The word "Comforter" is translated from the Greek word, parakletos, and comes from two Greek words, "para" and "kletos" meaning to "call to one's side."[1] The word parakletos can be translated into six different English words. Each word is a name for the Holy Spirit and illuminates a different aspect of the Spirit's ministry and His work in our lives.

1) Advocate: He stands for us and represents us.

2) Comforter: He gives compassion and relief in physical, mental, and emotional distress.

3) Counselor: He guides and teaches us in all matters of daily living.

4) Helper: He equips and empowers us to live and work.

5) Intercessor: He works to bring about harmony and reconciliation.

6) Strengthener: He gives us perseverance and endurance.

In these final hours, Jesus continued to comfort and reassure His disciples. He did so by explaining the work of the Comforter who would come:

John 16:8 . . . he will reprove the world of sin, and of righteousness, and of judgment

1 The Analytical Greek Lexicon, Harold Moulton, Grand Rapids: Zondervan, 1978, p. 303

John 16:13 . . .he will guide you into all truth

John 16:13 . . .he will show you things to come.

John 16:14 He shall glorify me

John 16:15. . .he shall take of mine, and shall show it unto you.

As Jesus brought His discourse to a close, He spoke to His disciples of His imminent departure:

John 16:16 A little while, and ye shall not see me: and again, a little while, and ye shall see me, because I go to the Father.

Once again, the Lord's words must have caused confusion among the disciples, as indicated by their questions:

John 16:17 . . .What is this that he saith unto us, A little while, and ye shall not see me: and again, a little while, and ye shall see me: and, Because I go to the Father?

A Little While

The book of John records that Jesus' departure was to take place in "a little while." Five times Jesus told His disciples of this time frame, and we're told the disciples wondered among themselves. Jesus, knowing their concern, addressed their fears and once again affirmed that what He was telling them would take place soon.

John 7:33 Then said Jesus unto them, Yet a little while am I with you, and then I go unto him that sent me.

John 12:35 Then Jesus said unto them, Yet a little while is the light with you. Walk while ye have the light, lest darkness come upon you: for he that walketh in darkness knoweth not whither he goeth.

John 13:33 Little children, yet a little while I am with you. Ye shall seek me: and as I said unto the Jews, Whither I go, ye cannot come; so now I say to you.

John 14:19 Yet a little while, and the world seeth me no more; but ye see me: because I live, ye shall live also.

John 16:16 A little while, and ye shall not see me: and again, a little while, and ye shall see me, because I go to the Father.

John 16:17 Then said some of his disciples among themselves, What is this that he saith unto us, A little while, and ye shall not see me: and again, a little while, and ye shall see me: and, Because I go to the Father?

John 16:19 Now Jesus knew that they were desirous to ask him, and said unto them, Do ye inquire among yourselves of that I said, A little while, and ye shall not see me: and again, a little while, and ye shall see me?

Once again, Jesus clearly told His disciples of things that would happen and the sorrow they would feel. He also reassured them that their sorrow would be turned to joy.

John 16:20, 22 Verily, verily, I say unto you, That ye shall weep and lament, but the world shall rejoice: and ye shall be sorrowful, but your sorrow shall be turned into joy. . .

And ye now therefore have sorrow: but I will see you again, and your heart shall rejoice, and your joy no man taketh from you.

Jesus promised that His joy could never be taken from them. Paul reminds us of this and proclaims the Lord's faithfulness in his letter to the church at Rome:

. . .neither death, nor life, nor angels, nor principalities, nor powers, nor things present, nor things to come, nor height, nor depth, nor any other creature, shall be able to separate us from the love of God, which is in Christ Jesus our Lord (Romans 8:38-39).

Our Joy is Secure in Jesus

Before turning His thoughts and words to His Father in prayer, Jesus once again comforted His disciples with words of love and assurance:

John 16:27-28 For the Father himself loveth you, because ye have loved me, and have believed that I came out from God. I came forth from the Father, and am come into the world: again, I leave the world, and go to the Father.

This time, the disciples understood and embraced His words. And their faith was strengthened.

John 16:29-30 His disciples said unto him, Lo, now speakest thou plainly, and speakest no proverb. Now are we sure that thou knowest all things, and needest not that any man should ask thee: by this we believe that thou camest forth from God.

Before Jesus began His prayer to His Father, He spoke about the rest that is found in Him alone and the victory that is His.

John 16:33 These things I have spoken unto you, that in me ye might have peace. In the world ye shall have tribulation: but be of good cheer; I have overcome the world.

With those final words to His disciples, Jesus lifted up His eyes to heaven and said,

Father. . .

NOW

O Father

Glorify

Thou Me with
Thine own self
with the

Glory

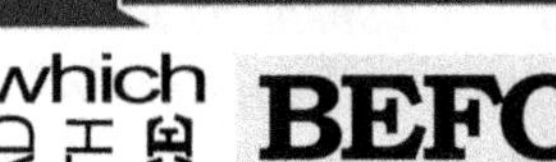

which I HAD WITH THEE

BEFORE
THE **world was.**

John 17:5

Chapter 5

Jesus Prayed

We now come to what I believe is the most precious passage in all of Scripture. While John 13-16 is a beautiful revelation of the very personal and intimate relationship between Jesus and His disciples, John 17 is the glorious culmination of the Upper Room's view of eternity. This chapter provides the greatest revelation of the unity, and the personal and intimate relationship, between God the Father and God the Son.

In this chapter are the words of Jesus, spoken to His Father in confident prayer, only hours before He would be betrayed. With this prayer, Jesus opened the eyes of His disciples to understand the unique relationship He eternally enjoys with His Father. And in His words, Jesus revealed the depths of His love and grace for them. The prayer also is a record of the blessings and gifts that will be given, after Jesus' death, burial, and resurrection, to those who are His.

Jesus prayed these precious words to His Father after the meal on the evening of Nisan 14. He first prayed about His disciples and then He prayed about all who would one day belong to Him. That means us! He prayed aloud in clear and simple words in the presence of His 11 faithful disciples for all to hear.

The entirety of this chapter is the real Lord's Prayer. Most Christians know the passage of Matthew 6:9-13 that the church calls, "The Lord's Prayer"—but that is not an accurate title. The prayer in Matthew 6 is a prayer that Jesus gave to His disciples to pray. He began, instructing them, "After this manner therefore pray. . ." (Matthew 6:9). The petitions of Matthew 6:12, asking for the forgiveness of sins, could not have been prayed by Jesus because He had no sins for which to be forgiven. The Matthew 6 prayer should really be titled "The Disciples' Prayer," and the title of "The Lord's Prayer" should be reserved for Jesus' prayer in John 17.

What is Prayer?

Prayer is an expression and practice of dependence on God and a way for us to experience unity and communion with Him. Prayer is a gift given to us by God that enables us to enter into His presence and talk to Him. Because we are "in Christ," we are told that we can come boldly before the throne of grace and "obtain mercy. . .and find grace" (Hebrews 4:16). In times of joy, we come before God with thanksgiving and praise. In times of trouble, we lay our problems at His feet and seek His will and direction, knowing that He will hear and will answer, comfort, and guide us.

Psalm 88:2 Let my prayer come before thee: incline thine ear unto my cry.

How should we pray?

Prayer must always begin in faith, believing that God hears, listens, cares, and answers. We know that God loves us and that He desires that we enter into a deep and abiding relationship with Him. Prayer is essential to doing that.

We must begin our prayers knowing that the Lord is good and gracious. The nature and desire of God is to give good things to His children, according to His divine will. Therefore, we can pray:

> *Matthew 6:9-10 After this manner therefore pray ye: Our Father which art in heaven, Hallowed be thy name. Thy kingdom come. Thy will be done in earth, as it is in heaven.*

We should desire what God desires because we know He is a good Father who loves us. The Lord's will being done on earth, as it is in Heaven, is our hope and prayer because God's will is perfect and good, and Holy (Hallowed) is his name.

We should always have trust and confidence because we know that whatever the Lord wills and commands us to do, He will also prepare and equip us to do (Philippians 2:13, Hebrews 13:21). By His Spirit, He will give us what we need to accomplish His work.

Pray with faith, confidence, and expectation.

Jesus knew that His Father heard His prayers; and He trusted in the goodness of His Father. He knew that He could ask anything of His Father. And He trusted that His Father would provide for His needs. Therefore, Jesus taught this to His disciples.

> *Matthew 6:8 . . .your Father knoweth what things ye have need of, before ye ask him.*

Matthew 21:22 And all things, whatsoever ye shall ask in prayer, believing, ye shall receive.

Mark 11:24 . . .What things soever ye desire, when ye pray, believe that ye receive them, and ye shall have them.

John 14:13-14 And whatsoever ye shall ask in my name, that will I do, that the Father may be glorified in the Son. If ye shall ask any thing in my name, I will do it.

Pray with openness and transparency.

Because God is omniscient, He knows all.

Matthew 10:26 . . .there is nothing covered, that shall not be revealed; and hid, that shall not be known.

Because God is omnipresent, He's everywhere and sees all.

Job 42:2 I know that thou canst do every thing, and that no thought can be withholden from thee.

Because God is omnipotent, all power is His.

Matthew 19:26 . . .With men this is impossible; but with God all things are possible.

Pray with humility and reverence.

When we understand God's holiness, we realize how lowly we are—and more importantly, how majestic He is.

- God is love and He is eternal.
- God is faithful, merciful, and true.
- God is omnipotent, omnipresent, and omniscient.
- God is transcendent, sovereign, and righteous.
- God is wise, just, and good.
- God is immutable, infinite, and incomprehensible.

When we remember these attributes of God, who "is before all things and by whom all things consist" (Colossians 1:17), then He is lifted up in our eyes, we are humbled before Him, and we will seek Him with due reverence, a grateful heart, a trusting faith, and a confident hope.

In Luke 18:9-13, Jesus told a parable of a Pharisee and a publican who prayed to God. The Pharisee prayed with pride and self-righteousness. The publican proclaimed himself a sinner in need of forgiveness and he prayed in humility. Jesus said of them:

> *Luke 18:14 I tell you, this man [the publican] went down to his house justified rather than the other [the Pharisee]: for every one that exalteth himself shall be abased; and he that humbleth himself shall be exalted.*

The bigger we see ourselves, the smaller we see our God. But the more we understand our sin, the more we will see our need for forgiveness, and the smaller we become and the bigger we see our God.

Pray with sincerity and simplicity.

Pouring out praises and petitions should not be done with embellishment, but with simplicity of true mindful thoughts and pure heartfelt emotions. God does not desire eloquent words and impressive intellectual oratory. He wants words that flow naturally from a heart of love, gratitude, and devotion. (Matthew 6:6-7).

Pray with your will being in accord with God's will.

Almost every prayer concludes with, "In Jesus' name, Amen." Praying "In Jesus' name" means that we are affirming it is in His power to hear our prayers and it is according to His perfect will that He will answer our prayers. The word amen is not just a closing word. It means "so be it." Therefore, it is an acknowledgment that we put our faith and trust in the Person of Jesus and in God's perfect purpose and plan for our lives.

When we truly believe and trust that God is good and that He gives abundantly, according to His character and nature, we would never want anything that is not in accordance with His will. (John 16:23-24)

For what should we pray?

We should pray *about* everything and we can pray *for* anything!

- In all things, we should give thanks to God (1 Thessalonians 5:18).
- In all things, we should bring our cares to the Lord (Psalm 55:22, 1 Peter 5:7), and
- In all things, we should present our petitions before the Lord (Matthew 7:7-8).

The following is a list of some general prayer suggestions. Please do not read these as prescriptive. And do not make them a "checklist" to be covered. There is no defined prescription for the way in which we should pray or for what we should pray. Prayer should always be a very personal communion with God. It should always be an offering to Him of what is on our minds and in our hearts. God already knows our thoughts and feelings, so come to Him in humble openness and honesty. Prayer should flow as freely from our hearts as a cascading waterfall or a river rushing to the sea.

Pray for growing sanctification.

Sanctification is the process of growing in holiness and becoming more and more conformed to the image of Jesus. It is the process that began the moment Jesus saved us and gave us the gift of His Holy Spirit to indwell us.

> *1 Thessalonians 5:18, 23 In every thing give thanks: for this is the will of God in Christ Jesus concerning you. And the very God of peace sanctify you wholly; and I pray*

God your whole spirit and soul and body be preserved blameless unto the coming of our Lord Jesus Christ.

Pray for forgiveness of sins.

We know that all of our sins—past, present, and future—have been forgiven. However, God still desires that we confess our sins and pray for forgiveness. It is a way of "washing our feet," as discussed in chapter 1 in the foot-washing passage of John 13. Our relationship with Jesus is secure, so our ongoing confession of sins is the way we keep our communion with Jesus "clean."

1 John 1:9 If we confess our sins, he is faithful and just to forgive us our sins, and to cleanse us from all unrighteousness.

Pray for the lost.

Jesus came to seek and save the lost (Luke 19:10) and, when He ascended to Heaven, His mission became our mission (John 17:18, Mark 16:15, Acts 26:18). Those who do not know Jesus need to be told about the love and saving grace of Jesus—and we need to pray for them.

1 Timothy 2:1 I exhort therefore, that, first of all, supplications, prayers, intercessions, and giving of thanks, be made for all men. . .

Pray for your service to God and your service to others.

We are to love God with all our heart, soul, mind, and strength and to love our neighbor as ourselves (Matthew 22:37, Mark 12:30-31, Luke 10:27). We are to be the Lord's laborers and we are to manifest our love for Him in service to others.

Matthew 9:37-38 Then saith he unto his disciples, The harvest truly is plenteous, but the labourers are few;

Pray ye therefore the Lord of the harvest, that he will send forth labourers into his harvest.

Acts 20:35 I have showed you all things, how that so labouring ye ought to support the weak, and to remember the words of the Lord Jesus, how he said, It is more blessed to give than to receive.

Galatians 6:9-10 And let us not be weary in well doing... As we have therefore opportunity, let us do good unto all...

Pray to forgive those who sin against you.

When we remember how much we have been forgiven, we will be quick to forgive those who have sinned against us.

Mark 11:25 And when ye stand praying, forgive, if ye have ought against any: that your Father also which is in heaven may forgive you your trespasses.

Ephesians 4:32 And be ye kind one to another, tenderhearted, forgiving one another, even as God for Christ's sake hath forgiven you.

Pray for your needs.

God will meet all of our needs. Jesus has told us to come to Him with our petitions.

Matthew 11:28 Come unto me, all ye that labor and are heavy laden, and I will give you rest.

Philippians 4:19 But my God shall supply all your need according to his riches in glory by Christ Jesus.

Pray for the needs of others.

We are to love others with the same kind of love that God

gives us. We should willingly listen to others, hear their needs, and respond with compassion , and pray for them.

John 13:34 A new commandment I give unto you, That ye love one another; as I have loved you, that ye also love one another.

1 Timothy 2:1 I exhort therefore, that, first of all, supplications, prayers, intercessions, and giving of thanks, be made for all men.

James 5:16 Confess your faults one to another, and pray one for another, that ye may be healed. The effectual fervent prayer of a righteous man availeth much.

Pray for protection against falling into temptation.

There is an enemy who seeks to devour us (1 Peter 5:8). And we still have a sin nature that can lead us into temptation. Therefore, pray for protection and strength to be faithful to God.

Matthew 26:41 Watch and pray, that ye enter not into temptation: the spirit indeed is willing, but the flesh is weak.

James 4:7 Submit yourselves therefore to God. Resist the devil, and he will flee from you.

1 Timothy 6:11 But thou, O man of God, flee these things; and follow after righteousness, godliness, faith, love, patience, meekness.

Why did Jesus pray?

Just as prayer is our means of communication with God, so also it was for Jesus in His humanity. When Jesus came to earth and took on human form, He set aside His divinity (Philippians 2:7). He did not live as God, although He remained fully divine. Therefore, living a human life, Jesus also prayed to His Father in Heaven. If Jesus had lived in His divinity (that's a hypothetical "if"), He could not have prayed. To whom would He have prayed? He would have been speaking to Himself, which would be thinking, not praying.

When did Jesus pray?

Jesus prayed daily.

The Jews prayed the Shema of Deuteronomy 6:4-5 daily and Jesus, as a devout Jew, would have done the same. Both Mark and Luke wrote of Jesus quoting the words of that Scripture.

> *Mark 12:29-30 And Jesus answered him, The first of all the commandments is, Hear, O Israel; The Lord our God is one Lord: And thou shalt love the Lord thy God with all thy heart, and with all thy soul, and with all thy mind, and with all thy strength: this is the first commandment.*

> *Luke 10:27 And he answering said, Thou shalt love the Lord thy God with all thy heart, and with all thy soul, and with all thy strength, and with all thy mind; and thy neighbour as thyself.*

Jesus prayed early in the morning.

While there is no specific time of day for prayer, rising early and starting one's day with prayer is both wise and prudent. The day can easily slip away. Plus, there is no better way to begin one's day than to come before the throne of God in prayer. It will center our hearts and focus our minds on Jesus.

> *Mark 1:35 And rising very early in the morning, while it was still dark, he departed and went out to a desolate place, and there he prayed.*

Jesus prayed with thanksgiving before eating.

All that we have is given by God, and that includes our daily sustenance for our physical bodies (James 1:17). Just as Jesus thanked His Father for the provision of food, we are to do the same.

> *Matthew 14:19 Then he ordered the crowds to sit down on the grass, and taking the five loaves and the two fish, he looked up to heaven and said a blessing. Then he broke the loaves and gave them to the disciples, and the disciples gave them to the crowds.*

> *Mark 14:23 And he took a cup, and when he had given thanks he gave it to them, and they all drank of it.*

> *Luke 22:19 And he took bread, and when he had given thanks, he broke it and gave it to them, saying, "This is my body, which is given for you. Do this in remembrance of me."*

Where did Jesus pray?

Jesus prayed publicly.

> *Luke 3:21 Now when all the people were baptized, and when Jesus also had been baptized and was praying, the heavens were opened.*

> *John 6:11 And Jesus took the loaves; and when he had given thanks, he distributed to the disciples, and the disciples to them that were set down; and likewise of the fishes as much as they would.*

> *John 11:41-42 So they took away the stone. And Jesus lifted up his eyes and said, "Father, I thank you that you have heard me. I knew that you always hear me, but I said this on account of the people standing around, that they may believe that you sent me."*

Jesus prayed privately.

> *Mark 1:35 And in the morning, rising up a great while*

before day, he went out, and departed into a solitary place, and there prayed.

Luke 9:18 "... he was praying alone..."

Luke 5:15-16 But now even more the report about him went abroad, and great crowds gathered to hear him and to be healed of their infirmities. But he would withdraw to desolate places and pray.

Luke 22:41 And he was withdrawn from them about a stone's cast, and kneeled down, and prayed

Jesus prayed in small groups.

Luke 9:28 Now about eight days after these sayings he took with him Peter and John and James and went up on the mountain to pray.

Jesus affirmed public prayer.

Luke 18:10-13 Two men went up into the temple to pray; the one a Pharisee, and the other a publican. The Pharisee stood and prayed thus with himself, God, I thank thee, that I am not as other men are, extortioners, unjust, adulterers, or even as this publican. I fast twice in the week, I give tithes of all that I possess. And the publican, standing afar off, would not lift up so much as his eyes unto heaven, but smote upon his breast, saying, God be merciful to me a sinner.

Prayer is not limited by location. God hears us wherever we are because He is omnipresent. Never be embarrassed or ashamed to bow your head, or close your eyes, in prayer.

For whom did Jesus pray?

Jesus prayed for all people. God loves all people and He desires that all will come to know Him (2 Peter 3:9).

Jesus prayed for his enemies.

Matthew 5:44 But I say to you, Love your enemies and pray for those who persecute you,

Luke 23:34 And Jesus said, "Father, forgive them, for they know not what they do." And they cast lots to divide his garments.

Jesus prayed for his friends.

Luke 22:31-32 "Simon, Simon, behold, Satan demanded to have you, that he might sift you like wheat, but I have prayed for you that your faith may not fail. And when you have turned again, strengthen your brothers."

Jesus prayed for children.

Matthew 19:13 Then children were brought to him that he might lay his hands on them and pray.

Jesus prayed for us.

John 17:20 Neither pray I for these alone, but for them also which shall believe on me through their word.

How did Jesus pray?

Jesus prayed Scripture.

Mark 15:34 And at the ninth hour Jesus cried with a loud voice, "Eloi, Eloi, lema sabachthani?" which means [Psalm 22:1], "My God, my God, why have you forsaken me?"

Jesus prayed long prayers.

Luke 6:12 In these days he went out to the mountain to pray, and all night he continued in prayer to God.

Jesus prayed short prayers.

Mark 6:41 And taking the five loaves and the two fish he looked up to heaven and said a blessing and broke the loaves and gave them to the disciples to set before the people.

Jesus prayed sorrowful prayers.

John 12:27-28 "Now is my soul troubled. And what shall I say? 'Father, save me from this hour'? But for this purpose I have come to this hour. Father, glorify your name." Then a voice came from heaven: "I have glorified it, and I will glorify it again."

Jesus prayed thankful prayers.

Matthew 11:25-26 At that time Jesus declared, "I thank You, Father, Lord of heaven and earth, that You have hidden these things from the wise and prudent and have revealed them to babes. Even so, Father, for so it seemed good in Your sight."

Mark 14:22-23 And as they were eating, Jesus took bread, blessed and broke it, and gave it to them and said, "Take, eat; this is My body." Then He took the cup, and when He had given thanks. . .

Jesus prayed surrendered to His Father.

Matthew 26:39 He went a little farther and fell on His face, and prayed, saying, "O My Father, if it is possible, let this cup pass from Me; nevertheless, not as I will, but as You will."

Jesus prayed with his dying breath.

Luke 23:46 Then Jesus, calling out with a loud voice, said, "Father, into your hands I commit my spirit!" And having said this he breathed his last.

Why should we pray?

We should pray because prayer is communion with God and because God wants to hear the desires of our hearts

(Matthew 7:7-11).

We should pray because when we pray, we are given the wonderful privilege of participating in the Lord's work. He will use His children to accomplish that which He ordains and purposes. We are instruments in His hands to work out His will.

We should pray because it is both a privilege and an honor to talk to our Father through prayer.

Finally, we should pray because we know God hears our prayers. We are talking with the One who will never turn a deaf ear.

> *1 John 5:14 And this is the confidence that we have in him, that, if we ask any thing according to his will, he heareth us.*

Let Us Pray

Come before God in prayer with reverence, gratitude, and confidence.

- Reverence for who He is, giving honor to His name.
- Gratitude for all that He has done for us.
- Confidence, knowing that we are His, our salvation is secure, and He has given us everything we need.

Remember that God loves us and desires to hear our concerns, our cares, our joys, and our thanksgiving.

> *1 Peter 5:7 Casting all your care upon him; for he careth for you.*

> *Psalm 100:4 Enter into his gates with thanksgiving, and into his courts with praise: be thankful unto him, and bless his name.*

In Christ we have the position of son-ship, which makes it possible for us to "enter into His gates. . ." and come "boldly before the throne" to "obtain mercy, and find grace to help in time of need" (Hebrews 4:16)

The Bible records many great prayers of saints who have gone before us. We can learn from their prayers and gain insight into how we should pray. But always remember, the best example of prayer was given by our Lord, when He said, "After this manner therefore pray ye . . ."

> *Our Father which art in heaven, Hallowed be thy name. Thy kingdom come. Thy will be done in earth, as it is in heaven. Give us this day our daily bread. And forgive us our debts, as we forgive our debtors. And lead us not into temptation, but deliver us from evil: For thine is the kingdom, and the power, and the glory, for ever. Amen. (Matthew 6:9-13)*

The High Priestly Prayer

As already stated, John 17 is the Lord's Prayer. It is a prayer that only the Lord Jesus could pray. John 17 is often referred to as the High Priestly Prayer, because it is a prayer of intercession by Jesus to His Father, on our behalf. Jesus is our High Priest, our intercessor to the Father (Hebrews 3:1).

Jesus was consecrated for this office on the day of His baptism by John the Baptist. Jesus' baptism was not of the baptism of John, which was a baptism for the remission of sins (Mark 1:4), "with water unto repentance" (Matthew 3:5). Jesus had no sins and therefore He had no need to be baptized "unto repentance."

When Jesus came to John, and John hailed Him as "the Lamb of God who takes away the sin of the world" (John 1:29), Jesus was preparing and presenting Himself for His public ministry. There is no dispute that this baptism was the beginning of Jesus' public ministry. Just as with all the Levitical priests, Jesus was consecrated by full immersion (baptism) in water (Leviticus 8:6). This fulfilled a righteous requirement of God for ministry service (Matthew 3:15).

We are told that when Jesus came up out of the waters of baptism, the Holy Spirit descended upon Him like a dove (Matthew 3:16, Mark 1:10, Luke 3:22). In the same way that kings and prophets were anointed with oil (the Spirit) to do God's work, Jesus received power from the Spirit to begin His public ministry. Jesus was also confirmed (consecrated and accepted) by His Father, when He said, "This is my beloved Son, in whom I am well pleased" (Matthew 3:17, Mark 1:11, Luke 3:22).

Jesus' baptism was His consecration for public ministry and the confirmation of the purpose of His ministry...to be the Lamb of God who would atone for man's sins and give good gifts to those who would come to Him in faith. John 17 reveals those gifts.

Holy Father

KEEP through

THINE OWN NAME

Those whom Thou Hast Given ME

THAT THEY

MAY BE

ONE AS WE ARE

John 17:11

Chapter 6

John 17
The Lord's Prayer

Let's now "enter into" the upper room. Let's "take a seat at the table" and "see" Jesus with the "eyes of our understanding" (Ephesians1:18). Let's hear His precious words as Scripture speaks to us.

The Bible tells us that Jesus prayed often, but nowhere in Scripture is His heart more tender, or His love more clearly revealed, than in this prayer. John 17 is exclusively the words of Jesus as He prayed to His Father. These words were spoken in the presence of his 11 faithful disciples, and they are recorded for the hearing of all God's people.

This prayer took place after the Passover meal and after Judas had departed. The words were spoken under the Old

Covenant—a covenant of promise and preparation. And that is exactly what Jesus had been doing in the upper room—revealing promises to His disciples and preparing them.

As Jesus prayed to His Father, those promises were clearly revealed. These promises would be given as gifts under the New Covenant. The New Covenant (New Testament), which would take effect with His death:

> *Hebrews 9:16-17 For where a testament is, there must also of necessity be the death of the testator. For a testament is of force after men are dead: otherwise it is of no strength at all while the testator liveth.*

Jesus' death instituted a new dispensation, no longer a time of promise and preparation. It began a time of fulfillment and possession.

Let's turn our thoughts to the most precious prayer in Scripture, The Lord's Prayer! The High Priestly Prayer! Let's picture in our minds the Lord Jesus Christ, with eyes raised to Heaven as He prayed. When Jesus began His prayer the meal was finished, and so also was His work on this earth:

> *John 17:4 I have glorified thee on the earth: I have finished the work which thou gavest me to do.*

Jesus had completed His earthly, public ministry of preparing God's people to recognize their Messiah. From the time John the Baptist announced Him as *"the Lamb of God, which taketh away the sin of the world"* (John 1:29), Jesus had taught them about their need for a perfect and final sacrifice for their sins. In less than 24 hours Jesus would become that sacrifice—a final substitutionary atonement for sinful man.

When Jesus had first announced that His hour had come (John 12:23), He declared *"for this cause came I unto this hour"* (John 12:27) and He petitioned His Father, *"glorify Thy name*" (John 12:28). To which the Father responded, *"I have both glorified it, and will glorify it again."* (John 12:28), and Jesus declared, *"This voice came not because of me, but for your sakes. . .And I, if I be lifted up from the earth, will draw all men unto me."* (John 12:30, 32)

The hour for which Jesus had come into this world was the hour of His death, and it was now before Him, and in these final hours Jesus declared, *". . .I have finished the work thou gavest me to do"* and He turned to His Father in prayer.

These Words Spake Jesus

> *John 17:1 These words spake Jesus, and lifted up his eyes to heaven, and said, Father, the hour is come; glorify thy Son, that thy Son also may glorify thee*

"These words spake Jesus. . ."

Jesus spoke aloud so all present would hear. It was Jesus' purpose, even in this prayer to His Father, to encourage and prepare His faithful followers for what was to come. He spoke plainly so His faithful disciples would understand his words.

Lifted Up His Eyes

"These words spake Jesus, and ***lifted up his eyes to heaven****"*

Jesus lifted up His eyes to Heaven. Isn't that what we are to do? Paul says that we are to focus our eyes on Jesus, the Author and Finisher of our faith (Hebrews 12:2), so we are to keep looking up.

Jesus left Heaven to come to earth. What a sacrifice that must have been! The God of all creation humbled Himself and came to earth, taking on human form. In His incarnation Jesus was fully God and fully man, but Jesus set aside His divine nature and power (Philippians 2:7) to become like us. Jesus lived His earthly life as a man, not as God. He lived completely dependent upon His Father for the direction of His mission and for the strength to accomplish it. Knowing what would soon come to pass, Jesus faced His final hours on earth by looking to His Father for strength.

Just as Jesus looked to Heaven, we should also remember where we are to look for the Divine strength we need. We are to keep our eyes on Jesus (Hebrews 12:2), knowing He will complete the good work He has begun in us (Philippians 1:6).

Heads Up

Lifting eyes to Heaven is not a prayer posture that many Christians practice, but it is a practice all should consider. The first record of Jesus looking upward to Heaven in prayer was when He blessed the five loaves and the two fishes at the feeding of the 5,000 (Luke 9:13). Another time was at the raising of Lazarus from the dead. Jesus began by giving thanks to His Father and proclaiming His Father's faithfulness in hearing His prayers. As He prayed, Jesus *"lifted up his eyes."*

> *John 11:41-2 Then they took away the stone from the place where the dead was laid. And Jesus lifted up his eyes, and said, Father, I thank thee that thou hast heard me. And I knew that thou hearest me always: but because of the people which stand by I said it, that they may believe that thou hast sent me.*

Praying with eyes lifted to Heaven, as Jesus did in Luke 9, John 11, and John 17, is a posture of seeking God and giving thanks. We know that our help comes from the Lord (Psalm 121:2) and we should look to Him to guide our lives.

> *Psalm 123:1 Unto thee lift I up mine eyes, O thou that dwellest in the heavens.*

Isaiah 40:26 Lift up your eyes on high, and behold who hath created these thing. . .

Hebrews 12:2 Looking unto Jesus the author and finisher of our faith. . .

In order to lift our eyes to Heaven, our head must be lifted up. In the psalms we read of the lifting-up of the head as being an indication of victory. David spoke of holding one's head high in triumph over his enemies. He spoke of this twice about himself:

Psalm 3:3 But thou, O LORD, art a shield for me; my glory, and the lifter up of mine head.

Psalm 27:6 And now shall mine head be lifted up above mine enemies round about me: therefore will I offer in his tabernacle sacrifices of joy; I will sing, yea, I will sing praises unto the LORD.

Again, in Psalm 110, David spoke of lifting-up the head. In this case his words were prophetic. He told of a promised Messiah who would come and reign. The Messiah would be both the Son of David and the Lord of David. He would be a Priest of the Most High God, not from human descent in the Levitical line but from the order of Melchizedek (Hebrews 5:6), the King of Righteousness. In Psalm 110, David closed by speaking of a coming Saviour King who would judge both kings and nations. David told that this great Victor would triumphantly hold his head high:

Psalm 110:7 He shall drink of the brook in the way: therefore shall He lift up the head.

Jesus' head was lifted-up, when He was resurrected and was fully glorified, when He ascended into Heaven and was seated at the right hand of the Father

Jesus is the Victor and our victory is in Him. The Christian life is a rhythm of daily "death" and "resurrection," of dying-to-self and being raised-up and strengthened by Jesus. When we seek Jesus, and turn our hearts toward Him, He will lift up our heads, and then we can set our eyes upon Him.

Try praying with your eyes lifted-up to Heaven, seeking the One who has promised to lift-up your head in victorious life.

> *Romans 8:37 . . .we are more than conquerors through him that loved us.*

Heads Down

Our traditional prayer posture is to pray with our heads bowed. A bowed head indicates a humble spirit and submission to God in reverence—as we should be.

In ancient days, a bowed head was the common posture with which to approach a king or a monarch. The posture acknowledged the nobleman's position and rule and the common person's submission to authority.

The book of Jeremiah speaks of God's command to the people of Israel to surrender their necks to the yoke of the King of Babylon. This means that they were to acknowledge and submit to his authority.

> *Jeremiah 27:8 And it shall come to pass, that the nation and kingdom which will not serve the same Nebuchadnezzar the king of Babylon, and that will not <u>put their neck under the yoke of the king of Babylon</u>, that nation will I punish, saith the LORD, with the sword, and with the famine, and with the pestilence, until I have consumed them by his hand.*

> *Jeremiah 27:12 I spake also to Zedekiah king of Judah according to all these words, saying, <u>Bring your necks under the yoke of the king of Babylon, and serve him and his people, and live.</u>*

Putting one's neck under the yoke required bowing the head in submission. God warned of the dangers of holding one's head high to blow one's horn and He commanded that His people not speak with a stiff neck.

> *Psalm 75:5 Lift not up your horn on high: speak not with a stiff neck.*

A stiff neck was an action of rebellion and a reflection of a hardened heart:

> *Deuteronomy 31:27 For I know thy rebellion, and thy stiff neck: behold, while I am yet alive with you this day, ye have been rebellious against the LORD; and how much more after my death?*

> *2 Chronicles 36:13 And he also rebelled against king Nebuchadnezzar, who had made him swear by God: but he stiffened his neck, and hardened his heart from turning unto the LORD God of Israel.*

> *Jeremiah 17:23 But they obeyed not, neither inclined their ear, but made their neck stiff, that they might not hear, nor receive instruction.*

God desires that we surrender our necks and come under Jesus' yoke—for His yoke is easy and His burden is light (Matthew 11:30). Bowing our heads in prayer, is a visible sign of respect, indicating we honor the rule and lordship of Jesus, and acknowledging His position as King of kings and Lord of lords. Bowing our heads in prayer expresses our desire to surrender and submit to His will.

Even Jesus, as He took His last breath, surrendered His neck to the will of His Father. He bowed His head and "gave up the ghost." He had willingly finished the work that His Father had sent Him to do—He had given His life to pay for the sins of the world.

John 19:30 When Jesus therefore had received the vinegar, he said, It is finished: and *he bowed his head,* *and gave up the ghost.*

Whatever prayer posture you use, head up and eyes lifted or head bowed and neck surrendered, remember that it should not be a legalistic practice. God is not concerned with our physical posture in prayer. It is the posture of our hearts that is important. God desires a heart of love and devotion, a spirit of humble surrender, and a desire of willing submission. Let's summarize:

- Lifting our eyes toward Heaven focuses our eyes on Jesus, and reminds us of our vertical relationship with Him and the glorious gifts that He has given us.
- Bowing our heads humbles our hearts and reminds us of our desperate need for Jesus and the importance of living in total dependence on Him.
- Lifting our eyes to Heaven is a posture of praise, adoration, and thanksgiving.
- Bowing our heads is a posture of worship, devotion and surrender.

The early church father Augustine wrote in his letter to Anicia that we should not begin to pray, asking for what we want, until we remember that in Christ we have all that we need. And so Jesus began His prayer remembering all that He had. . .unity with His Father.

"Father"

3) "These words spake Jesus. . . ***Father. . ."***

Jesus began His prayer with "Father," the name of God that signifies their intimate relationship. Jesus referred to God as Father more than 200 times, and five of those times are found here in this prayer: 1) verse 5, "O Father. . ." 2) verse 11, "Holy

Father. . ." 3) verse 21, "Father. . ." 4) verse 24, "Father. . ." and 5) verse 25, "Righteous Father. . ."

The Greek word for father in John 17 is "pater." There is also an Aramaic word for father, which Jesus used in Mark 14:36, "Abba."

> *Mark 14:36 And he said, Abba, Father, all things are possible unto thee; take away this cup from me: nevertheless not what I will, but what thou wilt.*

Translating the word "Abba" to "Father," we could read this in English as Father, Father. Repeating words was a common form of emphasis in biblical times (e.g. truly, truly or holy, holy, holy). Given the context of Jesus' request to His Father, it is understandable that He began with emphasis upon God being His loving Father. Throughout His life, Jesus sought the Father's will and demonstrated His confidence and trust in His Father's power, purpose and plan.

The apostle Paul also used the Aramaic word,"Abba," to describe our relationship with the Father in Galatians 4:6 and Romans 8:15. The intimate relationship of son-ship with the Father is given to us through adoption into God's family. Just as Jesus called God "Father," so also can we:

> *Romans 8:15 For ye have not received the spirit of bondage again to fear; but ye have received the Spirit of adoption, whereby we cry, Abba, Father.*

It is our great blessing that we can pray to God as *OUR* Father. We should pause to remember the significance of this. It is much more than just a salutation that speaks of our position as His child. God is Holy (John 17:11) and Righteous (John 17:25); and unlike any earthly father, He is perfect and will never disappoint us. In God, we can have total confidence and we can find true joy and lasting satisfaction. In

God we can have total confidence and we can find true joy and lasting satisfaction. Remembering these things, we are able to pray with heartfelt surrender and committed trust. We are able to pray, *"Our Father, who art in Heaven. . ."*

The Hour is Come

*4) "These words spake Jesus. . .**the hour is come. . .**"*

The hour, which had been promised in the Garden of Eden, had now come.

- This was the hour when the seed of the woman would bruise the head of the serpent and the serpent would bruise His heel (Genesis 3:15).
- This was the hour when the promised Rescuer would rescue His people from the curse and the wages of sin.
- This was the hour of which Jesus had spoken so many times (John 2:4, 7:30, 8:20, 12:23, 13:1).
- This was the hour of God's judgment of the sins of man.
- This was the hour of suffering for the Saviour.
- This was the hour of Jesus' victory over sin and death.
- This was the hour, planned and purposed by the Father.
- This was the hour that would fulfill the words of Isaiah.

"He will swallow up death in victory. . . (Isaiah 25:8)

This hour will forever be remembered by all believers as:

- The greatest demonstration of sacrificial love.
- The greatest gift ever given.
- The greatest gift ever received.

Paul echoed the words of Isaiah when He said:

"O death, where is thy sting? O grave, where is thy victory?" (1 Corinthians 15:55).

- In this hour, Jesus conquered death.
- In this hour, Jesus claimed victory.

- In this hour, Jesus opened the way to eternal life.

Only shortly before Jesus prayed the words, *"the hour is come,"* He had clearly told His disciples, *"I am the way, the truth and the life. . ."* (John 14:6).

Now, before the day would end, Jesus would defeat death and open the way to eternal life with Him. In the upper room, Jesus told His disciples exactly what His life, death, burial and resurrection would mean for them. In His prayer, He revealed the precious gifts that would be theirs.

Glorify Thy Son

5) *"These words spake Jesus. . .**glorify thy Son, that thy Son also may glorify thee."***

Jesus had come from glory. He had humbled Himself and taken on human form to live among His creation. He would soon be returning to the glory that He had known throughout all eternity. The Lord's petition was for the promised glory that He would soon receive through His work on the cross and the completion of His mission.

Jesus had come to be our mediator, to take upon Himself our sins and to offer Himself the perfect sacrifice that would atone for the sins of mankind. Jesus lived and died in total surrender and submission to the will of His Father, and in doing so He glorified His Father.

> *John 17:4 I have glorified thee on the earth: I have finished the work which thou gavest me to do.*

The glory spoken of is incomprehensible. Just as the Lord was glorified when He died and rose from death, so also we are given the promise of glory to come when we die.

The Bible gives us some revelation of the glory to come, but until we enter into that glory we cannot fully understand what it will be. It is so far beyond anything our minds can conceive or comprehend. All we can do is stand in awe of the glory that Jesus has promised us. We know that it will be a complete rest and we will have the joy of forever being in His presence. It will be the ultimate gift of the peace of God.

Peace *with* God and Peace *of* God

As believers, we have already been given peace *with* God. The Bible tells us that those who do not believe in Jesus are already condemned (John 3:18), but for those who have received His gift of salvation, they are now "in Him," and there is no condemnation (Romans 8:1). Jesus has forgiven our sins and given us His righteousness, making us worthy before God. Therefore, we have peace *with* God.

The ultimate and full peace of God is the restoration of the shalom (peace) that Adam and Eve knew and enjoyed prior to their sin. That peace will be the perfect shalom (peace) of God. It will be the perfect communion that God desired and designed into, His creation. For all believers, there will be a day, when we will enter into glory and enter into the fullness of God's peace. And for all creation, there will be a day, when the glory of the Lord will fill the whole earth (Habakkuk 2:14).

Paul wrote about the peace of God in Philippians 4.

> *Philippians 4:7And the peace of God, which passeth all understanding, shall keep your hearts and minds through Christ Jesus.*

While peace *with* God is positional (we have been given it in our justification), and it is unconditional and totally secure (we can never lose it), the peace *of* God is conditional. Peace *of* God is best understood as the peace we receive *from* God. It is the peace that is practical in our lives, meaning it is active, and can be experienced and evidenced in our lives. The peace *of* God is received. It is a fruit of the Spirit and is often most clearly felt in times of trouble when God quiets our minds, comforts our hearts, and settles our souls.

God is ever-willing to give us His peace. We receive it when we turn our hearts and minds to Him and remember His love and that He promises to work all things together for our good and for His glory.

Paul gave a prescriptive plan for renewing the mind that will open our hearts to receiving God's peace:

> *Philippians 4:8-9 Finally, brethren, whatsoever things are true, whatsoever things are honest, whatsoever things are just, whatsoever things are pure, whatsoever things are lovely, whatsoever things are of good report; if there be any virtue, and if there be any praise, think on these things. Those things, which ye have both learned, and received, and heard, and seen in me, do: and the God of peace shall be with you.*

When we "think on these things" and remember God's truth, faithfulness, justice, purity, love, and goodness, we can trust that God is with us and for us. By renewing the mind in this way, we receive the peace of God and we can find rest in even the most difficult of circumstances.

Remember that we have positional peace with God in our justification (when Christ saved us) and we can have the practical peace of God, in our sanctification (our Christian walk). Lifting our eyes to Heaven, as Jesus did in this prayer, keeping our focus on Jesus, and remembering all that He has done for us, all that He has given to us, and all of His precious promises, will strengthen us and give us His peace.

The Lord's Words and His Will–John 17

We've established that John 17 is the Lord's prayer—the words spoken by Jesus, from His heart to His Father. Let's examine Jesus' words in the context of this being His Last Will and Testament —a document that bequeaths His possessions to those He loves after His death.

Throughout history, people have drafted legal documents to express their wishes about how, and to whom, their possessions are to be distributed after their death. Their wishes are recorded by legal counsel and in the presence of witnesses. In this chapter, Jesus spoke to the only perfect legal counsel, the only perfectly just Judge, the One who has all authority and all rule over all things.

In ancient Israel, property and possessions passed from one generation to the next through the bloodline and according to Levitical law. The bequests that Jesus spoke in John 17 are passed to us in the same way. Every person who belongs to Jesus is washed in His blood (Revelation 1:5), and is a child of God and a joint-heir with Jesus (Romans 8:17).

Jesus also bequeathed in accordance with the Royal Law, as recorded in the book of James.

> *James 2:8 "If ye fulfill the royal law according to the scripture, Thou shalt love thy neighbor as thyself, ye do well."*

The Royal Law is described as the law of love. And just before Jesus prayed this prayer, He spoke of His great love for His disciples:

> *John 15:9 As the Father hath loved me, so have I loved you: continue ye in my love.*

In His love, Jesus bequeathed His most precious gifts to His faithful disciples and to all who would come to be His disciples. These are unmerited gifts given in love by His grace and they are far more valuable than gold and silver, and far more enduring than any worldly possessions.

The Greatest Prayer Ever Prayed

Jesus' prayer in John 17 is His longest recorded prayer. It is also the longest prayer recorded in the New Testament (only Solomon's prayer in 2 Chronicles 6:12-40 and Ezra's prayer in Nehemiah 9:4-37 are longer).

Certainly, we can say this prayer is the greatest prayer ever prayed on earth and also the greatest prayer recorded in Scripture. This prayer is often called the "Holy of Holies" of the gospel record. We must approach this "Holy of Holies" with humility and reverence, with gratitude and worship, with joy and thanksgiving, mindful of the Lord's abounding love and grace, spoken here and soon to be demonstrated.

- Consider what a great privilege it is to read the words of our Saviour as He prayed to His Father, shortly before He offered His life as a ransom for our sins.
- Consider what a blessing it is that He bequeathed to us all that we need to live our lives.
- And, most importantly, consider what a joy and hope it is to know Him, to love Him, and to trust Him.

If I could hear Christ praying for me in the next room, I would not fear a million enemies. Yet distance makes no difference. He is praying for me. —Robert Murray McCheyne (1813-1843)

God looks not. . .at the oratory of your prayers—how elegant they may be; nor at the geometry of your prayers—how long they may be; nor at the arithmetic of your prayers—how many they may be; not at logic of your prayers—how methodical they may be; but He looks at the sincerity of your prayers. —Thomas Brooks (1608-1680)

The Spirit Himself
bears witness
with our spirit
that we are
CHILDREN OF GOD
and if
CHILDREN
then heirs
heirs of God and joint heirs
WITH CHRIST
if indeed we suffer with Him, that we may also be
glorified together.
Romans 8:16-17

Chapter 7

The Last Will & Testament of the Lord Jesus Christ

I present for your consideration the view of eternity seen from the Upper Room. Read the words of Jesus in John 17 and consider that His words reveal His thoughts, His emotions, and His will, less than 24 hours prior to His death. Since we will look at these words as the Lord's Last Will and Testament, let's first understand what that is.

West's Encyclopedia of American Law defines a Last Will and Testament as: "

A fancy and redundant way of saying "will." Lawyers

> and clients like the formal resonance of the language. Will and testament mean the same thing. A document will be the "last" will if the maker of it dies before writing another one.[2]

The Baker Encyclopedia of the Bible offers a much longer definition of the word "testament:"

> English word translated from the Greek signifying the covenantal administrations of God: that prior to Christ being the "Old Testament" and that under Christ the "New Testament."
>
> The Greek word [diatheke], generally meaning "last will and testament," contains certain legal characteristics which have important theological implications. First, a testament was not an agreement between parties (especially equals), but rather was exercised solely by the testator. Second, the testament became effective upon the death of the testator. Third, the testament was irrevocable.
>
> When the OT was translated into Greek, the translators had the option of two words to translate the Hebrew word for covenant. One term carries the idea of a mutual agreement and this often between equals. Since this would blur the divine initiative in God's covenantal dealings with the patriarchs and with Israel, the other word was used. It connoted the self-determined action of the sovereign in making the covenant. The New Testament writers saw in the word testament an additional significance. As a testament became valid at the death of the testator, the benefits of the new covenant have come to believers after the crucifixion and the death of the Christ (Heb 9:15–22; cf. 1 Cor 11:25; Luke 22:20, KJV).[3]

---

2 West's Encyclopedia of American Law, edition 2. ©2008 The Gale Group, Inc

3 Walter A. Elwell and Barry J. Beitzel, Baker Encyclopedia of the Bible

The Bible records two primary covenants between God and man—the Old Covenant and the New Covenant. The Old Covenant was in effect prior to the cross of Jesus and the New Covenant since that time.

The Baker Encyclopedia states:

> It is not accidental that the two volumes of the Christian Bible have been called the Old Covenant and New Covenant.[4]

By definition the words will and testament mean the same thing. And, by definition, testament carries a meaning of:

> "agreement, binding agreement, contract, covenant, engagement, expression of conviction, formal declaration, legal will, promise, solemn agreement, solemn promise, testamentary declaration, testamentary decree, testamentum, will, writing." [5]

Since "testament" is another word for "covenant," we can understand that the laws, reproof, correction, and instructions recorded in the Old Testament were made by God, under the Old Covenant and with the nation of Israel, not with us. The words of the New Testament are under the New Covenant and apply to us.

Before moving on, we must understand that there was a transition period while Jesus was on earth. Although all four Gospel accounts are included in the New Testament, some of what they record was under the Old Covenant. It was only after the death of Jesus that the New Covenant (New Testament) came into effect.

We are also told in Scripture that the Old Covenant was until John the Baptist, confirming that a transition period existed during Jesus earthly ministry,

---

(Grand Rapids, MI: Baker Book House, 1988), 2046.

4 Ibid, 531.

5 http://legal-dictionary.thefreedictionary.com/testament

Luke 16:16 The law and the prophets [a common reference to the Old Testament/Covenant] were until John. . .

Considering the Old Covenant as the first Last Will and Testament, we'll accept that it was replaced with a new Last Will and Testament, that of the Lord Jesus Christ (the New Covenant).

Scripture tells that there was need for a new, second, and final covenant:

Hebrews 8:7 For if that first covenant had been faultless, then should no place have been sought for the second.

Hebrews 8:13 In that he saith, A new covenant, he hath made the first old. Now that which decayeth and waxeth old is ready to vanish away.

As we read Jesus' words in John 17, we will see how the words of this chapter meet the criteria of a Last Will and Testament.

Jesus is the Testator of the Will

West's Encyclopedia of American Law defines the testator of a will as:

> Testator, n. a person who has written a will which is in effect at the time of his/her death. A testator is a person who makes a valid will. A will is the document through which a deceased person disposes of his property. A person who dies without having made a will is said to have died intestate.
>
> A testator must be of sound mind when making a will. In part to ensure that a testator is of sound mind, states require that the signing of a will be witnessed by multiple persons. A testator also should be making the Will without duress and free of coercion from other persons.

> If the testator is not acting of his own free will in consenting to the terms of the Will, a court may later void all or part of it.[6]

Jesus met the criteria to be the Testator of this Will:

- Jesus was of sound mind.
- He clearly expressed His desires regarding the disposition of His property (possessions) following His death.
- His Last Will and Testament was verbally given before legal counsel (the Just Judge, God the Father).
- His Last Will and Testament was recorded so it could be read to those who are named as beneficiaries.
- The document was witnessed by multiple people and it was signed by the Testator (sealed in blood, as was the custom of those days).

The Gifts of God

We certainly think of the great gifts of forgiveness, justification, and eternal life that Jesus gives to those who come to Him in faith, but there is much more that He gives to those who receive Him. In studying the 26 verses of John 17, we can more fully understand the awesome and abundant grace of our God. He not only gives eternal life, starting the moment He saves a sinner, but also everything needed to live life *in* Him and *for* Him until the day one goes to Heaven.

It's important to understand how Jesus' life, death, burial, and resurrection brought forth the New Covenant (New Testament) under which we live.

Baker Encyclopedia's definition of the word "testament" lists the criteria required for a will to come into effect:

1) First, a testament was not an agreement between parties (especially equals), but rather was exercised solely by the

6 Ibid.

testator. [7]

As the Testator, Jesus solely exercised the New Testament.

Ephesians 2:8-9 For by grace are ye saved through faith; and that not of yourselves: it is the gift of God: Not of works, lest any man should boast.

2) Second, the testament became effective upon the death of the testator. 8

Hebrews 9:16 For where a testament [covenant] is, there must also of necessity be the death of the testator [Jesus].

3) Third, the testament was irrevocable.9

Romans 11:29 For the gifts and the calling of God are irrevocable.

Just as the legal document of a Testament is irrevocable, the gifts that the Lord Jesus Christ's bequeathed are also irrevocable! Our eternally security is guaranteed because we are sealed (Ephesians 4:30b, 2 Corinthians 1:21- 22). We are assured of our salvation in the Person of Jesus Christ, the Testator (John 10:28, Romans 8:38-39, 11:29, Jude 1:24), who wrote a new covenant, His Last Will and Testament. This Testament superseded any prior Testament (specifically, the Old Testament/Old Covenant).

His Will and Testament Proclaimed

Now, let's return to the upper room and listen as Jesus speaks His "Last Will and Testament." As He spoke, Jesus knew that His death was imminent and His Will (testament) would only take effect after His death:

Hebrews 9:17 For a testament is of force after men are

7 Ibid.
8 Ibid.
9 Ibid.

dead: otherwise it is of no strength at all while the testator liveth.

- It was Jesus' perfect, sinless life on earth that made Him the perfect, sinless Lamb of God—the only one who could conquer death.

John 10:10 . . .I am come that they might have life, and that they might have it more abundantly.

- It was Jesus' death that opened the way of salvation, by paying the penalty for man's sin.

Hebrews 9:26, . . .he appeared to put away sin by the sacrifice of Himself.

- It was Jesus' resurrection that conquered death and restored His glory.

John 17:1 These words spake Jesus, and lifted up his eyes to heaven, and said, Father, the hour is come; glorify thy Son, that thy Son also may glorify thee:

In this prayer, Jesus prayed for all who would come to Him in faith. His words are for those who would trust in Him, be saved by Him, and be adopted into the family of God—because only they are rightful heirs.

John 17:9 I pray for them: I pray not for the world, but for them which thou hast given me; for they are thine.

In John 17:1, when Jesus spoke of the hour having come, He spoke not of His death but of His glorification. Jesus would soon be restored to the place of glory, Heaven, but, additionally, He would also be glorified. This means that He would be lifted up, elevated, honored, magnified, and exalted. The hour that was to come was the hour of glory because His death would pay the debt of mankind's sin and open the way to glory with God. Jesus would be glorified because of His perfect submission to the will of His Father and because of His finished work on the cross. Knowing the glory to come enabled Jesus to find joy in His suffering:

> *Hebrews 12:2 . . .Jesus the author and finisher of our faith; who for the joy that was set before him endured the cross. . .*

As Jesus "lifted His eyes" (John 17:1) He looked upward to His Father and He looked forward to His glory—the hope and promise of what was to come. With the cross in "sight," He looked toward the crown. Let this be a pattern for our lives and in our prayers.

Through the Cross to the Light

I have a cross necklace formed with the Latin phrase:

Per Crucem ad Lucem

The English translation is:

"Through the Cross to the Light"

The words are a reminder that Jesus is the Light of the World who came into a dark world, and through His death we find light and life.

> *Psalm 112:4 Unto the upright there arises light in the darkness: he is gracious, and full of compassion, and righteous.*

> *Psalm 97:11 Light is sown for the righteous, and gladness for the upright in heart.*

We must always remember *per crucem ad lucem*—through the cross to the Light.

- It *was* through the cross that Jesus paid for sin, conquered death, and defeated Satan.
- It *was* through the cross that the way to the Father was opened.
- It *was* through the cross that Jesus received the crown.
- It *is* through the cross that we have Light in this life and glorious Light to come.

The cross was not a tragedy. It was a triumph. It was only through the agony of the cross that Jesus was glorified and it is through the cross that we come to the Light and find joy in this life and look forward to unspeakable joy in the next.

In all we do, we should lift our eyes to Jesus. We should look to the Author and Finisher of our faith (Hebrews 12:2) and remember the promise of glory, the joy that is set before us.

The Gifts of the Testator

Scripture contains many promises given by Jesus, but none so precious as the gifts He promised in His prayer.

The gifts we inherit include, salvation (verse 2) , manifestation (verse 6), representation (verse 9), preservation (verse 12), sanctification (verses 17-19), identification (verses 21), and glorification (verse 22).

Before we read John 17 as the Lord's Last Will and Testament, let's establish what is His full name. Often we only use the name Jesus, or we call Him by the titles of Lord or Christ. But we should understand that His full name is triune in nature—The Lord Jesus Christ. The first mention of this full name is found in Acts.

> *Acts 11:17 Forasmuch then as God gave them the like gift as he did unto us, who believed on the Lord Jesus Christ. . .*

The triune name proclaims 1) His title—Lord, 2) His given, human name—Jesus, and 3) His office—Christ (Messiah).

He is the Son of Abraham—the King of the Jews.

He is the Son of David—the King of kings.

He is the Son of Man—the Lord of lords.

He is the Son of God—the King of glory

He is the Son of Righteousness (Malachi 4:2)

He is the Name above all names—the Lord Jesus Christ.

And, He is the rightful owner of all the gifts He bequeathes.

Jesus' words in John 17 tell of the immeasurable gifts of grace and eternal life, along with the special gifts for righteous living, that Jesus has bequeathed to His own.

Now, as Jesus said, in the Gospels of Matthew, Mark, and Luke, and in Revelation—"He that hath an ear, let him hear."

The Last Will & Testament of the Lord Jesus Christ

THE BEQUESTS

1) Eternal Life

John 17:2 As thou hast given him power over all flesh, that he should give eternal life to as many as thou hast given him.

John 17:24 Father, I will that they also, whom thou hast given me, be with me where I am; that they may behold my glory, which thou hast given me: for thou lovedst me before the foundation of the world.

2) My Words

John 17:8 For I have given unto them the words which thou gavest me; and they have received them, and have known surely that I came out from thee, and they have believed that thou didst send me.

John 17:14 I have given them thy word; and the world hath hated them, because they are not of the world, even as I am not of the world.

3) My Joy

John 17:13 And now come I to thee; and these things I speak in the world, that they might have my joy fulfilled in themselves.

4) My Protection

John 17:15 I pray not that thou shouldest take them out of the world, but that thou shouldest keep them from the evil.

5) My Mission

John 17:18 As thou hast sent me into the world, even so have I also sent them into the world.

6) My Glory

John 17:22 And the glory which thou gavest me I have given them; that they may be one, even as we are one.

7) My Love

John 17:26 And I have declared unto them thy name, and will declare it: that the love wherewith thou hast loved me may be in them, and I in them.

THE WITNESSES

For a Testament to be legal, there must be witnesses. In biblical times two witnesses were required by law; and, in the case of Jesus' testament, there were two human, two divine, and two personal witnesses.

Deuteronomy 19:15 One witness shall not rise up against . . .at the mouth of two witnesses, or at the mouth of three witnesses, shall the matter be established.

Matthew 18:16 . . .take with thee one or two more, that in the mouth of two or three witnesses every word may be established.

Two Human Witnesses

1) John the Baptist

John 1:29 The next day John seeth Jesus coming unto him, and saith, Behold the Lamb of God, which taketh away the sin of the world.

2) The Disciples

John 15:27 And ye also shall bear witness, because ye have been with me from the beginning.

Acts 10:39 And we are witnesses of all things which he did both in the land of the Jews, and in Jerusalem; whom they slew and hanged on a tree:

Two Divine Witnesses

1) The Father

Matthew 3:17 And lo a voice from heaven, saying, This is my beloved Son, in whom I am well pleased.

2) The Scriptures

John 5:39 Search the scriptures; for in them ye think ye have eternal life: and they are they which testify of me.

Two Personal Witnesses

1) Jesus' Words

John 18:37 Pilate therefore said unto him, Art thou a king then? Jesus answered, Thou sayest that I am a king. To this end was I born, and for this cause came I into the world, that I should bear witness unto the truth. Every one that is of the truth heareth my voice.

2) Jesus' Works

John 5:36 But I have greater witness than that of John: for the works which the Father hath given me to finish, the same works that I do, bear witness of me, that the Father hath sent me.

THE SEAL OF THE TESTAMENT

Jesus' Blood

Matthew 26:28 For this is my blood of the new testament, which is shed for many for the remission of sins.

THE EXECUTOR OF THE TESTAMENT

The Holy Spirit

John 15:26 But when the Comforter is come, whom I will send unto you from the Father, even the Spirit of truth, which proceedeth from the Father, he shall testify of me:

THE RESPONSIBILITIES OF THE EXECUTOR

1) Alert those who are included in the Will.
2) Witness to the existence of the Will.
3) Have the Will published following the testator's death.
4) Make provisions for the dispensation of the gifts bequeathed in the Will.

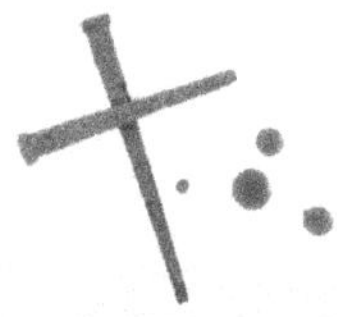

KEEP through

THINE OWN NAME

Those whom Thou Hast Given ME

THAT THEY

MAY BE

ONE AS WE ARE

Chapter 8

Probating the Will

In chapter 7, we read John 17 as the Last Will and Testament of the Lord Jesus Christ. Now we will focus on a new beginning when the Will was administered.

Following the death of a Testator, a Will must first be established (validated). Then the process of administering the Will begins. The Will is read (or a copy given) to those who are named as beneficiaries and the desires of the deceased person are declared. Distribution of the gifts bequeathed is then administered by the person appointed as executor of the Will, and the beneficiaries receive their inheritance.

Jesus spoke His Last Will and Testament to the Almighty Judge who has power and authority to probate the Will (probate is a legal term that means to verify that a Will is valid). The apostle John also confirmed the Will when he wrote his epistles.

The Will Confirmed in John's Epistles

The apostle John recorded the words that Jesus spoke in the upper room so that we might believe.

> *John 20:31 ..these are written, that ye might believe that Jesus is the Christ, the Son of God; and that believing ye might have life through his name.*

God has graciously preserved these words for almost 2,000 years. What a great blessing for us!

We *reflect* on the words we read, but John *heard* these words as he sat at Jesus' right hand and leaned back upon His bosom (John 13:23). John heard every precious word spoken—words of comfort, hope, and joy— and some 50+ years later, the Holy Spirit brought them to his mind and he recorded them in his gospel account—the Book of John.

John not only recorded the gifts in his Gospel, he also confirmed each gift in the epistles that he wrote shortly after. Again, he did this so that we might believe by knowing:

> *1 John 5:13 These things have I written unto you that believe on the name of the Son of God; that ye may know that ye have eternal life, and that ye may believe on the name of the Son of God.*

Let's compare Jesus' words in His High Priestly prayer to John's words in his three letters.

The Gifts

1) Eternal Life:

> *John 17:2 As thou hast given him power over all flesh, that he should give eternal life to as many as thou hast given him.*

Jesus alone has the power to give life. Prior to the life, death, burial, and resurrection of Jesus, the people lived trying to keep the Law of God hoping for a righteousness they could never attain. The Law was good, and it instructed them in righteous living, but the Law had no power to save them It did however reveal how far short of God's perfect standard they were and served to help them see their need for a Saviour. Jesus came to seek and save the lost (Luke 19:10) and to be the Life-giver to all who come to Him in faith. This gift is confirmed in the apostle John's first epistle:

> *1 John 2:25 And this is the promise that he hath promised us, even eternal life.*

> *1 John 5:11 And this is the record, that God hath given to us eternal life, and this life is in his Son.*

> *1 John 5:13 These things have I written unto you that believe on the name of the Son of God; that ye may know that ye have eternal life, and that ye may believe on the name of the Son of God.*

2) The Lord's Words:

> *John 17:8 For I have given unto them the words which thou gavest me; and they have received them, and have known surely that I came out from thee, and they have believed that thou didst send me.*

> *John 17:14 I have given them thy word; and the world hath hated them, because they are not of the world, even as I am not of the world.*

Jesus' words strengthen, deepen, and increase our faith. His words enrich our lives and give us hope and rest. Romans 10:17 tells us that "faith comes by hearing, and hearing by the word of God." We have been given the great gift of the Bible, God's Word, and from it, we receive knowledge, wisdom, and discernment. The Word of God also gives us hope and comfort to strengthen us in trials and tribulations, and direction to guide us in our thoughts, words, and actions.

The Word of God is the Sword of the Spirit and it reveals the power of God living in us and through us. Take up your Sword by spending time reading and studying the Bible. Go forth into the world with the power of the Sword (Hebrews 4:12) and never lay down your Sword.

The receiving of Jesus' words that He bequeathed to us in John 17 is confirmed by the apostle John in his first epistle:

> *1 John 2:14 I have written unto you, fathers, because ye have known him that is from the beginning. I have written unto you, young men, because ye are strong, and the word of God abideth in you, and ye have overcome the wicked one.*

3) The Lord's Joy:

> *John 17:13 And now come I to thee; and these things I speak in the world, that they might have my joy fulfilled in themselves.*

Because we have received eternal life, our joy is abundant. Jesus told us that His words would sustain this gift of joy:

> *John 15:11 These things have I spoken unto you, that my joy might remain in you, and that your joy might be full.*

John confirmed this in his first epistle:

> *1 John 1:4 And these things write we unto you, that your joy may be full.*

4) The Lord's Protection

John 17:15 I pray not that thou shouldest take them out of the world, but that thou shouldest keep them from the evil.

Jesus prayed for protection prior to bequeathing His mission. When Jesus commissioned the disciples in Matthew 10, He had warned that the message they would carry would bring danger and division. He told them that He had not come to bring peace, but a sword and that "man would be set against father, daughter against mother, and daughter in law against mother in law; and a man's foes shall be of his own household" (Matthew 10:34-35). As dangerous as the mission was, Jesus told them ". . .he that loses his life for my sake shall find it" (Matthew 10:39). God's protection is given to us.

John confirmed this in his first epistle:

1 John 4:4 Ye are of God, little children, and have overcome them: because greater is he that is in you, than he that is in the world.

5) The Lord's Mission

John 17:18 As thou hast sent me into the world, even so have I also sent them into the world.

Jesus was sent by His Father "to preach the gospel to the poor. . .to heal the brokenhearted, to preach deliverance to the captives, and recovering of sight to the blind, to set at liberty them that are bruised. . .to preach the acceptable year of the Lord" (Luke 4:18-19). Our thankfulness to God for what He has given us should be so great that our mission should be fueled by a love for Jesus and love for others. Our mission is to tell others of the gifts the Lord desires to give them. If we love our neighbors, we will tell them about Jesus.

John confirmed this in his first epistle:

1 John 3:23 And this is his commandment, That we should believe on the name of his Son Jesus Christ, and love one another, as he gave us commandment.

6) The Lord's Glory

John 17:22 And the glory which thou gavest me [illegible] given them; that they may be one, even as we are one.

The glory that Jesus has, and that He has given to us, is union with God. Through His saving grace, we have been made one with our Triune God. Remember that our glory, our union with God, began the moment that Jesus saved us.

John confirmed this in his first epistle:

1 John 1:3 That which we have seen and heard declare we unto you, that ye also may have fellowship with us: and truly our fellowship is with the Father, and with his Son Jesus Christ.

1 John 4:16 And we have known and believed the love that God hath to us. God is love; and he that dwelleth in love dwelleth in God, and God in him.

7) The Lord's Love

John 17:26 And I have declared unto them thy name, and will declare it: that the love wherewith thou hast loved me may be in them, and I in them.

While we struggle to comprehend the amazing love of God, the awe that it generates is both assuring and comforting. We are told of God's love for Jesus when the Father declared Him to be His beloved Son (Matthew 3:17). Jesus declared He had the love of the Father in John 17:26 and Paul also affirmed it when he gave Jesus the title of Beloved in his letter to the Ephesians (verse 1:6). Because Jesus is the object of the

Father's love, and because we are in Christ, we also are the recipients of the love of God the Father.

John confirmed that we have received God's love in his first epistle:

> *1 John 3:1 Behold, what manner of love the Father hath bestowed upon us, that we should be called the sons of God: therefore the world knoweth us not, because it knew him not.*

> *1 John 4:9 In this was manifested the love of God toward us, because that God sent his only begotten Son into the world, that we might live through him.*

The Lord's Peace

This final gift was given while Jesus was still with them. It was given to them through the words He spoke to them:

> *John 14:27 Peace I leave with you, my peace I give unto you: not as the world giveth, give I unto you. Let not your heart be troubled, neither let it be afraid.*

> *John 16:33 These things I have spoken unto you, that in me ye might have peace. In the world ye shall have tribulation: but be of good cheer; I have overcome the world.*

The Lord's peace was given to them to comfort them in their sorrow and strengthen them when they felt alone. This gift was not mentioned in Jesus' prayer and yet the peace of God is embedded in each and every gift that Jesus bequeathed. It is the peace we have that comes from our union with God and it grows when we trust in Christ. The apostle Paul tells us this peace "surpasses all understanding, [and] will guard [our] hearts and minds through Christ Jesus." (Philippians 4:7) John reminds us of this peace in his first epistle:

1 John 4:18 There is no fear in love; but perfect love casteth out fear. . .

1 John 5:5 Who is he that overcometh the world, but he that believeth that Jesus is the Son of God?

The Witnesses

The human witnesses were confirmed by John:

1 John 4:14 And we [John and the disciples] have seen and do testify that the Father sent the Son to be the Saviour of the world.

3 John 1:12 Demetrius hath good report of all men, and of the truth itself: yea, and we also bear record; and ye know that our record is true.

The Divine witnesses were confirmed by John:

1 John 5:6 This is he that came by water and blood, even Jesus Christ; not by water only, but by water and blood. And it is the Spirit that beareth witness, because the Spirit is truth.

1 John 5:7 For there are three that bear record in heaven, the Father, the Word [the Son] and the Holy Ghost: and these three are one.

1 John 5:8 And there are three that bear witness in earth, the Spirit, and the water, and the blood: and these three agree in one.

1 John 5:9 If we receive the witness of men, the witness of God is greater: for this is the witness of God which he hath testified of his Son.

The Responsibilities of the Executor

Finally, John confirmed each of the responsibilities of the Holy Spirit in His job of executing the will:

1) Alert those who are included in the will.

1 John 1:2 (For the life was manifested, and we have seen it, and bear witness, and show unto you that eternal life, which was with the Father, and was manifested unto us;)

2) Witness to the existence of the will.

1 John 1:1 That which was from the beginning, which we have heard, which we have seen with our eyes, which we have looked upon, and our hands have handled, of the Word of life

3) Have the will published following the testator's death.

1 John 1:3 That which we have seen and heard declare we unto you, that ye also may have fellowship with us: and truly our fellowship is with the Father, and with his Son Jesus Christ.

1 John 1:5 This then is the message which we have heard of him, and declare unto you, that God is light, and in him is no darkness at all.

4) Make provisions for dispensation of the gifts bequeathed.

1 John 1:4 And these things write we unto you, that your joy may be full.

1 John 4:13 Hereby know we that we dwell in him, and he in us, because he hath given us of his Spirit.

1 John 5:11 And this is the record, that God hath given to us eternal life, and this life is in his Son.

1 John 5:13 These things have I written unto you. . .that ye may know that ye have eternal life, and that ye may believe on the name of the Son of God.

1 John 5:20 And we know that the Son of God is come, and hath given us an understanding, that we may know him that is true, and we are in him that is true, even in his Son Jesus Christ. This is the true God, and eternal life.

Three Questions

When Jesus died, the Will came into effect, and fifty-three days later, the Holy Spirit was sent to execute the Will and to distribute the gifts to Jesus' heirs.

There remain three questions that you must ask yourself:

1. Are you in Jesus' Will as a beneficiary?
2. Have you read the Will?
3. Have you received your inheritance?

Are you in the Will?

If there has been a time in your life when you turned to Jesus in faith and asked Him to forgive your sins, then you have been saved. The Bible tells "that if you confess with your mouth the Lord Jesus and believe in your heart that God has raised Him from the dead, you will be saved" (Romans 10:9).

Have you read the Will?

The Apostle John, by the power of the Holy Spirit, has recorded the words of Jesus. Read John 17 often. It is a wonderful reminder for us of our glorious inheritance of both justification (eternal life with Jesus) and the many gifts in our sanctification (growing in holiness).

Have you received your inheritance?

It is by grace we have been saved and by faith that we now live. Truly believing and trusting in the One who has given these gifts makes them real and effectual in our daily lives.

"Now, since these promises of God are words of holiness, truth, righteousness, liberty, and peace, and are full of universal goodness, the soul, which cleaves to them with a firm faith, is so united to them, thoroughly absorbed by them, that it not only partakes in, but is penetrated and saturated by, all their virtues." — Martin Luther

Standing on the promises of Christ my King,
Through eternal ages let His praises ring,
Glory in the highest, I will shout and sing,
Standing on the promises of God.

Standing on the promises of Christ the Lord,
Bound to Him eternally by love's strong cord,
Overcoming daily with the Spirit's sword,
Standing on the promises of God.

Standing on the promises I cannot fall,
Listening every moment to the Spirit's call
Resting in my Savior as my all in all,
Standing on the promises of God.

~ Standing On The Promises
Kelso Carter, 1886

CHRIST IN YOU, THE *Hope* OF Glory

Epilogue

Living the Promises

We receive the promises of the Lord's life, words, joy, protection, mission, glory, and love the moment we are saved, but how do we live the promises on a daily basis? Let's look at each gift individually, but before doing so, let's consider the first question of the Westminster Shorter Catechism, "What is the chief end of man?" This can be re-phrased with a more contemporary emphasis to ask, "What is my purpose in life?" The catechism's simple answer is, "to glorify God and enjoy Him forever."

That answer remains true today. It is the secret to living in the promised gifts that we have already received.

How, as Christians, should we live and how can we truly feel the presence of Jesus in our daily lives and share His love with others. It begins in the heart and in the mind. We must choose to devote our hearts to Jesus, and we must dedicate ourselves to renewing our minds in the Word of God. Doing both of those glorifies God and produces in us a life of rest and an enjoyment in God that's unending and unbounded.

Jesus is both our Saviour and our Sustainer. He saved us and regenerated our souls, and He also supplies that which we need to live.

Let's consider how we can live for Jesus by living in His-promises and enjoying the gifts He has given us. Let's look at each of the bequests that Jesus spoke in His Last Will and Testament.

1) Eternal Life:

> *John 17:2 As thou hast given him power over all flesh, that he should give eternal life to as many as thou hast given him.*

Life everlasting is the glory that awaits us but it's also the blessing of inheritance that we received the moment Jesus saved us. Trusting that we have eternal life gives us joy in the present and the hope of a greater joy to come when we will see Jesus face-to-face and behold the glory of God.

> *John 17:24 Father, I will that they also, whom thou hast given me, be with me where I am; that they may behold my glory, which thou hast given me: for thou lovedst me before the foundation of the world.*

2) The Lord's Words:

> *John 17:8 For I have given unto them the words which thou gavest me; and they have received them, and have known surely that I came out from thee, and they have believed that thou didst send me.*

> *John 17:14 I have given them thy word; and the world hath hated them, because they are not of the world, even as I am not of the world.*

The true, holy, and perfect words of God have been given to us. They pierced our souls when Jesus saved us and they continue to transform our minds every time we read them.

Living the promise and the gift of His words means spending time reading and studying the Bible. It is necessary for the fullness of life in Christ.

3) The Lord's Joy:

> *John 17:13 And now come I to thee; and these things I speak in the world, that they might have my joy fulfilled in themselves.*

Jesus has given us His joy as a fruit of the Spirit and yet in His prayer he said that we might have it fulfilled. Living this gift is a choice. We must choose joy. We choose to have it fulfilled in us by letting the Lord's words and His gifts of life and joy reign in our hearts. It is a joy that is not conditioned on worldly circumstances but on the steadfast love of our God that is eternally ours and we are eternally His.

4) The Lord's Protection

> *John 17:15 I pray not that thou shouldest take them out of the world, but that thou shouldest keep them from the evil.*

We know that we live in a world that is not our home. It is a world that denies the truths of God and desires to follow fleshly and ungodly ways. In this gift, Jesus asks the Father to protect us in the world. We are told to walk in the Spirit and to avoid the temptations of the flesh. In doing so, we become vulnerable to the desires of the evil one to destroy us. But Jesus has given us His protection:

> *John 16:33 These things I have spoken unto you, that in me ye might have peace. In the world ye shall have tribulation: but be of good cheer; I have overcome the world.*

> *1 John 5:4 For whatsoever is born of God overcometh the*

world: and this is the victory that overcometh the world, even our faith.

1 John 5:5 Who is he that overcometh the world, but he that believeth that Jesus is the Son of God?

Rom 8:31 ...If God be for us, who can be against us?

Rom 8:37 ...we are more than conquerors through him that loved us.

5) The Lord's Mission

John 17:18 As thou hast sent me into the world, even so have I also sent them into the world.

Knowing that we are secure in our life in Christ, free to choose to be joyful, and protected in our pilgrimage on this earth, we can move forward in the mission that Jesus has given us. It is a privilege and the life's work of every Christian to help grow the spiritual Kingdom of God here on earth.

As Christians, we are all called to share the gospel of saving grace with the lost; and we are also called to share the gospel of sanctifying grace with brothers and sisters in Christ.

6) The Lord's Glory

John 17:22 And the glory which thou gavest me I have given them; that they may be one, even as we are one.

Jesus says He has given us His glory and for a very specific purpose—to unite us as one together with each other. We are united in Christ by the power of the Holy Spirit. And we are united as His body, each part having its own important role in the overall functioning of the body. Symbolic as the picture of the body is, it is helpful for us in remembering that when one part of "the body" is "injured" or "burdened" other parts of the body must take over and compensate until the "injured" is restored. Living in the glory which Jesus has given us is living in unity with others in His Body.

Jesus has given us many symbolic images to explain our union together and in Him—the Body, the Bride, the Branches of the Vine—all intended to help us more fully understand a spiritual union while we remain in this physical world

7) The Lord's Love

John 17:26 And I have declared unto them thy name, and will declare it: that the love wherewith thou hast loved me may be in them, and I in them.

It's interesting that Jesus "bequeathed" eternal life, and His words, joy, protection, mission, and glory before He "bequeathed" love. Perhaps it's because the greatest of these gifts is love. In love for us, Jesus gave every other gift and, in this last gift, He gives the love of the Father that it may be in us.

It is an unending love, a perfect love, a joyous love, a protective love, a giving love, a uniting love. It's a love that exceeds our understanding and yet it is ours. It's a love that satisfies in ways we cannot imagine, and yet we have it. It is a love that empowers us to live as pilgrims on this earth, knowing that our true home is in Heaven. And it is a love that fills and fulfills—over and over, and over again.

How do we live the promises, the gifts of John 17? In Him and by Him, in love!

1 John 4:9 In this was manifested the love of God toward us, because that God sent his only begotten Son into the world, that we might live through him.

1 John 4:11 Beloved, if God so loved us, we ought also to love one another.

The Spirit Himself
bears witness
with our spirit
that we are
CHILDREN OF GOD
and if
CHILDREN
then heirs
heirs of God and joint heirs
WITH CHRIST
if indeed we suffer with Him, that we may also be
glorified together.
Romans 8:16-17

Sharing the Promises

As Christians we have been commissioned to share our faith with those who do not know Jesus. Read about the three strand cord and use it to open spiritual conversations to share the love of Jesus.

A Three Stand Cord

A three strand cord is strong. It is not easily broken. (Ecclesiastes 4:12). So also the saving grace found only in Jesus Christ is strong and it has a strong three-fold assurance that it can never be broken.

A black strand reminds us of our sin. In the Bible black symbolizes sin and death.

There is none righteous; all have sinned and fall short of the glory of God. (Romans 3:10, 23)

For the wages of sin is death; but the gift of God is eternal life through Jesus Christ our Lord. (Romans 6:23)

A gold strand reminds us of the love of God. In the Bible gold symbolizes deity. Gold is a precious metal of great value and desire. It reminds us of the precious and valuable gift of God's love for us and His love given to us.

For God so loved the world, that he gave his only begotten Son, that whosoever believeth in him should not perish, but have everlasting life. (John 3:16)

A red strand reminds us of the blood of Christ, shed for our sins. In the Bible red symbolizes atonement. We are told that the life of man is in the blood and that blood must be shed to make atonement for man's sin.

For the life of the flesh is in the blood: and I have given it to you upon the altar to make an atonement for your souls: for it is the blood that maketh an atonement for the soul. (Leviticus 17:11)

Without shedding of blood there is no remission [of sin]; Christ died for our sins. . .was buried. . .was raised on the third day (Hebrews 9:22, 1 Corinthians 15:3-4)

Three-fold Blessing

The Bible proclaims the love, mercy and grace of the Triune God, and His three-fold blessing of promise and assurance.

1) God loved the world and and sent His Son to pay for the sins of mankind
2) God promises forgiveness and salvation to all who turn to Jesus and put their trust in Him.
3) God is faithful and His gift is forever.

"And I give them eternal life, and they shall never perish; neither shall anyone snatch them out of My hand. My Father, who has given them to Me, is greater than all; and no one is able to snatch them out of My Father's hand. I and My Father are one." John 10:28-30 (NKJV)

The Most Important Questions You'll Ever Answer

Are your sins forgiven? If you don't know Jesus, repent of your sins today. Confess them and ask Jesus for forgiveness. Turn to Him, and trust that He loves you and that He paid the penalty for your sins.

We are all only one heartbeat away from taking our last breath and stepping into eternity. Jesus promises that He has prepared a place for all who belong to Him.

> *"Let not your heart be; you believe in God, believe also in Me. In My Father's house are many mansions; if it were not so, I would have told you. I go to prepare a place for you. And if I go and prepare a place for you, I will come again and receive you to Myself; that where I am, there you may be also. And where I go you know, and the way you know." Jesus said. . ."I am the way, the truth, and the life. No one comes to the Father except through Me. John 14:1-4,6 (NKJV)*

Take a few minutes and search your heart. Think about the God of the universe, who loves you and came to earth to seek and save sinners. He lived the perfect, sinless life we cannot live. He died the brutal, cursed death that we should die. He paid the price for sin and He offers eternal life to all who come to Him in faith.

If you desire to know Jesus, turn to Him in prayer. Pray a prayer of repentance and trust, believing on His name. When you do so, He is faithful to do as He has promised. The apostle John confirms this in both his Gospel account and in his first epistle.

> *John 1:12 But as many as received him, to them gave he power to become the sons of God, even to them that believe on his name:*

John 20:31 But these are written, that ye might believe that Jesus is the Christ, the Son of God; and that believing ye might have life through his name.

1 John 5:13 These things have I written unto you that believe on the name of the Son of God; that ye may know that ye have eternal life, and that ye may believe on the name of the Son of God.

Examine your heart and see yourself as you are—a sinner in need of a Saviour. If you have never trusted in Jesus and received His gifts, pray now. Ask Jesus to forgive your sins and to give you everlasting life. Let your heart speak. Use your own words, or pray something like this:

> Lord Jesus, I know that I have sinned and that I am not worthy of your forgiveness. But the Bible tells me that you died to forgive all my sins, and that You promise, if I turn from my sin and trust in you, you will grant me forgiveness. I profess that I believe you died for my sins and that you rose from the dead. I desire to know You, and I ask that you forgive my sins and grant me eternal life; and help me to live my life in a way that pleases You. In Your name I pray. Amen.

If you prayed that prayer, asking Jesus to forgive you and believing on His name, welcome to the family of God. As a child of God, you are blessed, chosen, adopted, made alive, saved, raised up, accepted, redeemed, enlightened, and an heir of inheritance (Ephesians 1:3-5, 7, 9, 11). Live in the riches of your inheritance.

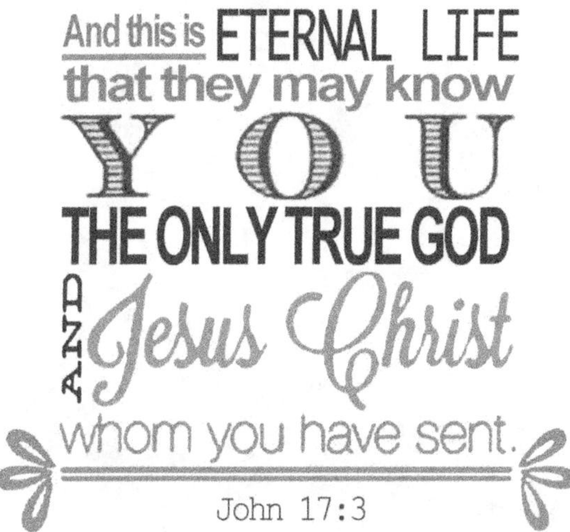
And this is ETERNAL LIFE
that they may know
YOU
THE ONLY TRUE GOD
AND Jesus Christ
whom you have sent.
John 17:3

A Final Thought

Jesus lifted His eyes to Heaven (John 17:1).

We can learn much from those six words. Ask yourself, where are you looking? It's important because where you look will determine what you see. And what you see will enter your mind, and what your mind thinks will direct your life.

The Light of the World

When Jesus saved us our eyes were opened. We received the many gifts of our inheritance, including the gift of the Holy Spirit by whom we have a clear view of eternity. He teaches us God's Word and reveals to us the mysteries of the riches of Christ. Until the day we go to Heaven to be with Jesus, we are told to keep looking up and to be watching.

> *Luke 21:27-28 And then shall they see the Son of man coming in a cloud with power and great glory. And when these things begin to come to pass, then look up, and lift up your heads; for your redemption draweth nigh.*

> *Titus 2:13 Looking for that blessed hope, and the glorious appearing of the great God and our Saviour Jesus Christ.*

Looking Up

The book of John tells us that Jesus is the Light of the world and all who follow Him have the light of life (John 8:12). Yet, in His incarnation, Jesus, the Light of the Word, looked up. His eyes were continually focused on God the Father, and His will was always surrendered to the will of the Father. As Christians we have the Light of Christ in us by the power of the Holy Spirit. And we are told to be always looking to the Light, for when we do so we are able to surrender to God's will.

> *Hebrews 12:2a looking unto Jesus the author and finisher of our faith. . .*

We should also consider why Jesus continually looked to His Father. Hebrews 12:2b tells that Jesus knew what was to come—His glorification and His return to His heavenly home. It was Jesus' hope of glory, His confident expectation of His exaltation to come, that gave Jesus strength to endure the cross.

> *Hebrews 12:2b . . .who for the joy that was set before Him endured the cross, despising the shame, and is set down at the right hand of the throne of God.*

Having the same hope of glory, the same confident expectation of our home in Heaven, is what gives us the strength to endure all tribulations, tests, trials, sorrows, pain, and suffering in our lives.

> *Colossians 1:27 To whom God would make known what is the riches of the glory of this mystery among the Gentiles; which is Christ in you, the hope of glory*

Why is a butterfly on the back cover?

Because butterflies are the best symbol of resurrection found in nature. The following is an excerpt from my first book, *Why the Butterfly? Rightly Remembering Jesus.*

"Why the Butterfly?"

The butterfly has long been recognized as a symbol of resurrection and hope. In the life cycle of a butterfly is a beautiful illustration of all phases of a redeemed person's life.

Every butterfly goes through four stages of development: egg, larva, pupa (or chrysalis), and adult butterfly. This process of development is called metamorphosis.

The life-cycle begins when the adult female lays her eggs on the underside of a leaf, which will later be a source of food for the caterpillar. The egg hatches into a larva, or caterpillar, looking very much like a worm.

Interestingly, in Psalm 22 David likens man to a worm, and Jesus, when speaking of the unredeemed in eternal torment, three times said, *"where their worm dieth not. . ."* (Mark 9:44, 46, 48).

This worm-like creature, the caterpillar, crawls on the ground, dependent on the earth for its sustenance and existence. This can be likened unto people who live seeking to fulfill worldly desires and obtain temporal possessions. Caterpillars eat continuously and voraciously—another parallel to man's appetite for worldly gain, which will never fully satisfy the soul.

The next phase of a caterpillar's life begins as it attaches itself upside down to a twig and sheds its skin—growing in its place a pupa or chrysalis, commonly called a cocoon. This cocoon clearly resembles a type of entombment or bondage. Take note that during ancient times, dead bodies were wrapped in burial cloths and then buried or entombed. The swaddling of the body, in preparation for burial during biblical times, is pictorially similar to the cocoon "wrapping" of the caterpillar. So the cocoon can be seen to represent death and also to the bondage of sin that brings death.

Inside the well sealed cocoon, the caterpillar does not feed and does not appear to be alive (another representation of death). However, in this phase, a transformation is occurring. The caterpillar is being transformed into a butterfly by a process called metamorphosis. In the next stage, the butterfly emerges from the confinement of its cocoon into the world, wet and with soft wings (symbolic of birth). Before the butterfly can fly, it must rest, allowing its body to dry and wings to harden (symbolic of rest in Christ and growing in faith). Then the butterfly takes flight, living the remainder of its life cycle between the earth and heaven and feeding on some of God's most beautiful creations — flowering plants.

As Christians, we also have gone through a metamorphosis. Beginning as an earthly worm (Job 25:6), followed by a death-to-self and a resurrection to new life in Christ (Romans 6:4-5, Galatians 2:20).

Just as God rested after creation and just as rest is necessary for the butterfly after its new birth, an important first step in our walk with the Lord is to learn to rest, or abide, in Christ (John 15:4- 11). Just as this rest is necessary for the butterfly's wings to dry and harden before it begins to fly, our rest in Christ strengthen us in our Christian walk.

A Christian's life begins with a metamorphosis, from death-to-self into eternal life with Christ, but it is also an ongoing process of transformation. Paul speaks of this:

> *And be not conformed to this world: but* ***be ye transformed by the renewing of your mind****, that ye may prove what is that good, and acceptable, and perfect, will of God. (Romans 12:2, emphasis added)*

The Greek word for transformed used in Romans 12:2, is "metamorphoo," from which we get metamorphosis—the process through which a caterpillar transforms into a butterfly. Just as we are transformed into a new creation in Christ (2 Corinthians 5:17), so also are we *being* transformed daily to be more and more like Jesus (Romans 8:29) and Paul tells us this is by the renewing of our minds.

Understand the distinction Paul is making here. Being "conformed to this world," is something that takes place from the outside, in. Being "transformed" is a change that takes place from the inside, out. This word, "metamorphoo," is also used in Matthew 17:2 and Mark 9:2 when Christ was transfigured and shone in all His glory, appearing to Peter, James and John.

The Glory Before us

Paul also speaks of our final metamorphosis, our final transformation, when Christ returns — our bodily resurrection to glory:

> *Behold, I show you a mystery; We shall not all sleep, but we shall all be changed, In a moment, in the twinkling of an eye, at the last trump: for the trumpet shall sound, and the dead shall be raised incorruptible, and we shall be changed. (1 Corinthians 15:51-52)*

> *But we all, with open face beholding as in a glass the glory of the Lord, are changed [metamorphoo] into the same image from glory to glory, even as by the Spirit of the Lord. (2 Corinthians 3:18)*

It interesting that in ancient Greece the word for soul, psyche ('ψυχή'), was also used for butterfly. Aristotle's Historia Animalium and Pliny's Naturalis Historia discuss "psyche" as representing both "butterfly" and "soul.

In the Greek culture, a butterfly was symbolic of the soul because of the butterfly's transformation (metamorphosis) from a caterpillar to a butterfly.

The butterfly is a beautiful reminder of our victory in Christ— victory over sin and death, and resurrection to new life by our only true Hope, Jesus Christ.

Turn Your Eyes Upon Jesus

In Christ, we are a new creation being conformed to His image. Keep looking up for our Blessed Hope! One day, He will come for us, His Bride (Titus 2:13), and, oh, what a glorious day that will be!

Turn your eyes upon Jesus
Look full in His wonderful face
And the things of earth will grow strangely dim
In the light of His glory and grace.
(Lyrics by Helen H. Lemmel, 1922)

May the God of hope
fill you with all
Joy and Peace
in believing, so that by
power of the Holy Spirit
you may abound
in hope.

Romans 15:13

NOW THIS IS

ETERNAL LIFE

THAT THEY MAY

KNOW YOU

THE ONE TRUE GOD, AND

JESUS CHRIST

WHOM YOU HAVE SENT.

JOHN 17:3

Appendix

John 17

John 17:1 These words spake Jesus, and lifted up his eyes to heaven, and said, Father, the hour is come; glorify thy Son, that thy Son also may glorify thee: [2] As thou hast given him power over all flesh, that he should give eternal life to as many as thou hast given him. [3] And this is life eternal, that they might know thee the only true God, and Jesus Christ, whom thou hast sent. [4] I have glorified thee on the earth: I have finished the work which thou gavest me to do. [5] And now, O Father, glorify thou me with thine own self with the glory which I had with thee before the world was. [6] I have manifested thy name unto the men which thou gavest me out of the world: thine they were, and thou gavest them me; and they have kept thy word. [7] Now they have known that all things whatsoever thou hast given me are of thee. [8] For I have given unto them the words which thou gavest me; and they have received them, and have known surely that I came out from thee, and they have believed that thou didst send me. [9] I pray for them: I pray not for the world, but for them which thou hast given me; for they are thine. [10] And all mine are thine, and thine are mine; and I am glorified in them. [11] And now I am no more in the world, but these are in the world, and I come to thee. Holy Father, keep through thine own name those whom thou hast given me, that they may be one, as we are. [12] While I was with them in the world, I kept them in thy name: those that thou gavest me I have kept, and none of them is lost, but the son of perdition; that the scripture might be fulfilled. [13] And now come I to thee; and these things I speak in the world, that they might have my joy fulfilled in themselves. [14] I have given them thy word; and the world hath hated them, because they are not of the world, even as I am not of the world. [15] I pray not that thou shouldest take them out of the world, but that thou shouldest keep them from the evil. [16] They are not of the world, even as I am not of the world. [17] Sanctify them through thy truth: thy word is truth. [18] As thou hast sent me into the world, even so have I also sent them into the world. [19] And for their sakes I sanctify myself, that they also might be sanctified through the truth. [20] Neither pray I for these alone, but for them also which shall believe on me through their word; [21] That they all may be one; as thou, Father, art in me, and I in thee, that they also may be one in us: that the world may believe that thou hast sent me. [22] And the glory which thou gavest me I have given them; that they may be one, even as we are one: [23] I in them, and thou in me, that they may be made perfect in one; and that the world may know that thou hast sent me, and hast loved them, as thou hast loved me. [24] Father, I will that they also, whom thou hast given me, be with me where I am; that they may behold my glory, which thou hast given me: for thou lovedst me before the foundation of the world. [25] O righteous Father, the world hath not known thee: but I have known thee, and these have known that thou hast sent me. [26] And I have declared unto them thy name, and will declare it: that the love wherewith thou hast loved me may be in them, and I in them.

The Feasts of the Lord

And the LORD spoke unto Moses, saying, Speak unto the children of Israel, and say unto them, Concerning the feasts of the LORD, which you shall proclaim to be holy convocations, even these are my feasts. Six days shall work be done: but the seventh day is the sabbath of rest, a holy convocation; you shall do no work therein: it is the sabbath of the LORD in all your dwellings. These are the feasts of the LORD, even holy convocations, which ye shall proclaim in their seasons. (Leviticus 23:1-4)

There were three feasts of the Lord:

1) The Feast of Passover,
2) The Feast of Shavuot, and
3) The Feast of Sukkot (Tabernacles).

Let's look at the feasts, leaving Passover for last.

The Feast of Shavuot

The second of the three feasts was the Feast of Shavuot. It is also called the Feast of the Harvest, and most commonly the Feast of Weeks. It was set by counting 50 days from the second day of Passover. This 50-day time period is called the Counting of the Omer. An omer is a unit of measure and, in this case, it was a unit of measure of the barley harvest. On the second day of Passover, an omer of barley was cut down and brought to the Temple as an offering.

At the end of the 50 days was the Feast of Shavuot, occurring at the time of the wheat harvest in early summer. In Greek, this feast is called Pentekkostos, which means 50, and it is transliterated into English as Pentecost.

With the wheat harvest offering symbolic of the Church, it is believed that this feast was partially fulfilled with the Ascension of Christ and the birth of the Church on the day of Pentecost, but it is yet to be completely fulfilled.

Exodus 34:22 And thou shalt observe the feast of weeks, of the firstfruits of wheat harvest, and the feast of ingathering at the year's end.

The Feast of Sukkot (Tabernacles)

The third appointed time on the Jewish calendar is the Feast of Ingathering, more commonly called the Feast of Tabernacles. This feast takes place at the end of the agricultural year, in early fall—at the time of the fruit harvest. The seven-day festival includes the Feast of Trumpets, Yom Kippur (The Day of Atonement), and the Feast of Sukkot (Tabernacles)

Exodus 23:16 And the feast of harvest, the firstfruits of thy labours, which thou hast sown in the field: and the feast of ingathering, which is in the end of the year, when thou hast gathered in thy labours out of the field.

The Feast of the Passover

Leviticus 23:5-6 In the fourteenth day of the first month at even is the Lord's passover. And on the fifteenth day of the same month is the feast of unleavened bread unto the LORD: seven days ye must eat unleavened bread.

The Feast of Passover was the first of the three feasts. It began on the fourteenth day of the month of Nisan, which was called the Day of Preparation. The Feast of Passover was a seven-day festival intended for the people to remember what

God had done for them in the Exodus from Egypt.

On the Day of Preparation, the people prepared their homes, their food, and their hearts for the Feast of Unleavened Bread, which was commanded by God to take place on the evening of Nisan 15 (Leviticus 23:6, above).

The First Passover

The first Passover meal took place in Egypt. After God's people had been in Egypt for 430 years (Exodus 12:40-41), the Lord began His plan to deliver them from Egyptian bondage and to set them on a journey to the land that He had promised to their father Abraham.

God raised up Moses and sent him to Egypt's Pharaoh with the petition, "let my people go" (Exodus 5:1, et al.). Ten times Pharaoh refused to release the people of Israel. With each refusal, God brought a plague upon Egypt and its people. The plagues included,

1. water turned to blood (Ex 7:14–25),
2. frogs (Ex 7:25–8:11),
3. lice (Ex 8:16–19),
4. flies (Ex 8:20–32),
5. disease and death of livestock (Ex 9:1–7),
6. boils upon man (Ex 9:8–12),
7. thunder and hail (Ex 9:13–35),
8. locusts (Ex 10:1–20),
9. darkness (Ex 10:21–29) and
10. the death of firstborn (Ex 11:1–12:36)

In each of these plagues, God protected His people. In God's protection of Israel from the tenth and final plague, we find prophetic types and patterns that point to God's promised Deliverer who would be Israel's Messiah—Jesus Christ—who would someday come to rescue God's people and deliver them from the bondage of sin.

The Tenth and Final Plague

The tenth plague was the most devastating. It was the plague of death in which every firstborn son in the land of Egypt would die.

> *Exodus 11:5 And all the firstborn in the land of Egypt shall die, from the firstborn of Pharaoh who sits upon his throne, even unto the firstborn of the maidservant that is behind the mill; and all the firstborn of beasts.*

God gave a provision to protect His people from this plague.

Preparing Their Homes, the Food, and Their Hearts

God instructed His people what they were to do on the Day of Preparation.

1. Prepare their homes.

They were told to remove all leaven, which is representative of sin, and sweep their homes clean.

2. Prepare the food.

Each household was to select a pure and spotless lamb on the 10th of Nisan. They were to keep the lambs at their homes for four days and kill them on the 14th day of the same month. When the lambs were killed, they were to drain the blood into a basin and prepare the animal to be eaten. They were to take the blood and "strike it on the two side posts and on the upper door post of the houses, wherein they shall eat it. . ." (Exodus 12:7). This provided a protective covering; and when the angel of death came, he would pass over all houses that were covered by blood. Additionally, they were to cook and eat the sacrificed lamb that same night.

3. Prepare their hearts.

The commands God gave for the Day of Preparation were meant to create trust and devotion in the people's hearts and prepare them to celebrate the Feast.

The Feast of Unleavened Breaded.

After the Day of Preparation, the people celebrated the Passover feast, and while they ate, God's judgment came upon the land of Egypt.

Exodus 12:29 And it came to pass, that at midnight the LORD smote all the firstborn in the land of Egypt, from the firstborn of Pharaoh that sat on his throne unto the firstborn of the captive that was in the dungeon; and all the firstborn of cattle.

Pharaoh's Response

Having witnessed the wrath of Israel's God, and overwhelmed with grief over the death of his son, Pharaoh released the people of Israel and sent them out from the land of Egypt. Although Pharaoh sent them out, it was God who actually led them out. He directed their way to the Red Sea. He led them to a place where they were hemmed in by the sea. Being pursued by the Egyptian army, and with no course of escape, God again provided for His People. He miraculously parted the waters of the sea and gave them safe passage to the other side. God then released His restraining hand upon the waters and the sea flowed freely again, drowning the armies of Pharaoh as they attempted to pursue the Israelites (Exodus 14). In doing all this, God preserved His people and they began their journey through the wilderness, which would eventually lead them to the Promised Land.

Remember the Passover

God told His people to observe the Passover Feast annually as a practice of remembrance of what He had done for them.

Exodus 12:14 And this day shall be unto you for a memorial; and ye shall keep it a feast to the LORD through-

out your generations; ye shall keep it a feast by an ordinance for ever.

Exodus 12:24-25 And ye shall observe this thing for an ordinance to thee and to thy sons for ever. And it shall come to pass, when ye be come to the land which the LORD will give you, according as he hath promised, that ye shall keep this service.

God commanded His people to partake of this feast every year to remember what He had done and to remind them that He would continue to love and provide for them. Observing this feast would forever bring to mind the Lord's protection and deliverance of His people and His faithfulness to continue loving and providing for them

Exodus 12:26-27 And it shall come to pass, when your children shall say unto you, What mean ye by this service? That ye shall say, It is the sacrifice of the LORD'S passover, who passed over the houses of the children of Israel in Egypt, when he smote the Egyptians, and delivered our houses. And the people bowed the head and worshipped.

The book of Leviticus mandates this feast (Leviticus 23:5) and gives additional information.

A New Calendar

At the time of the first Passover, God also "reset" the Israelites' calendar. Abib, which had been the seventh month on the calendar, became the first month. It should be noted that the name of the month, Abib, was later changed to Nisan, meaning "their flight." This name change occurred after the Babylonian captivity (See Nehemiah 2:1). Nisan is the commonly used name today, but remember that at the time of the exodus from Egypt the first month was called Abib.

> *Exodus 12:2, 13:4 This month shall be unto you the beginning of months: it shall be the first month of the year to you. This day came ye out in the month Abib.*

This change in the calendar began a two-calendar system for the nation of Israel. The religious calendar began with Abib (later Nisan) in the spring and the civil calendar with Tishri (early fall).

This introduction of a religious calendar was to mark a newness of life in God's people—a newness that was linked to the blood of the Passover lamb.

the
Gifts
of God
for the
People
of God

The Lord's Last Supper

The meal Jesus shared with His disciples is often called "The Last Supper." To this day it is commemorated annually by Christians worldwide on the Thursday before Easter. The day is commonly referred to as Maundy Thursday.

I remember as a child thinking that Maundy Thursday meant we were celebrating Monday through Thursday. After all, Palm Sunday had a special name. So did Good Friday. And of course, Sunday we call Easter. So why wouldn't we have a name for the days between Palm Sunday and Good Friday? Maundy (Monday) Thursday seemed to make sense to me. Maundy Thursday was the name of the last days Jesus spent with His disciples. My reasoning was pretty good, but my answer was completely wrong.

The word "maundy" has no connection to the word "Monday." It's not a variation of the spelling, nor is it a mispronunciation of Monday.

"Maundy" is a word that derives from the Latin word "mandatum," from which we get the English word mandate. A mandate is an official order, a commission, a decree, a directive, or a command. During Jesus' last supper with His disciples, Jesus gave them a mandate to remember His death.

He also mandated (decreed) a new commandment. Three times Jesus commissioned His disciples with the command to "love one another" (John 13:34, 15:12, 15:17).

Jesus' last supper with His disciples was famously rendered in oils, in the 16th century, by artist Leonardo da Vinci. da Vinci's painting accurately depicts Jesus with all 12 of His disciples present. It should be understood that the painting depicts the time during the meal. It does not depict the time after the meal when Jesus prayed (John 17). At that time, Jesus spoke only to His 11 faithful disciples for Judas had departed. (John 13:30)

As Christians, we agree that we are to celebrate the Lord's Last Supper according to Jesus' mandate to remember His death. But we should also remember the mandate to "love one another" that Jesus proclaimed three-times Jesus clearly told that people will know we are His disciples by the love we show for others (John 13:35). Maybe we should call this day Mandate Thursday so we remember the Lord's great love for us and that we are to reflect His love by loving others.

Devotion Begins by Remembering

The hymnist Robert Robinson wrote of the "wandering heart" in his hymn, "Come Thou Fount of Every Blessing"

(1758). Both a reminder and a warning, Robinson's lyrics proclaim, "Prone to wander, Lord, I feel it, Prone to leave the God I love..."

We must ask, why would any believer wander from such a gracious and loving God? The only reason is that they forget. They fail to remember who God is. His gracious works fade from memory, and their identity becomes anchored in the world instead of the only One who is our true and faithful hope.

In recent years some have called these wandering Christians grace amnesiacs, or identity amnesiacs. Both are very appropriate labels for Christians who have forgotten what they have already received and who they are in Christ. When we fail to remember, we are prone to wandering. When we wander, we forget and when we forget, we eventually fall.

However, when we remember the Lord's goodness, grace, and mercy, we will always return and find our rest in Him.

Robinson's beautiful hymn reminds all believers of the remedy for wandering. It is simply returning to Jesus, and so Robinson penned, "Here's my heart, O take and seal it, Seal it for Thy courts above."

"In Remembrance of Me"

Remembering was important to Jesus, and it must be important to us.

When Jesus told the disciples to partake of wine and bread and said, "do this in remembrance of me," He used the Greek word "anamnesis," which simply means "recollection." "Recall these things," He said to them. And this was not just a suggestion; it was an explicit command. He gave this command to protect them, and to protect all who would be His. The world attempts to turn the Lord's own away from Him and to lure them to follow after worldly gain and pleasure. As God's children, we must always remember that the things of this world are temporal and they have no power to save, sanctify, or satisfy. Only God can save and satisfy the soul, and only God can sanctify the mind and fill the heart with endless love.

The Greek word translated as the remembrance that the Holy Spirit gives to us (John 14:26) is "hupomimnesko." This word means to remind quietly, suggest to the memory, put in mind, bring to remembrance. While Jesus commanded us to remember His work, He also promised to help us. He has given us the Holy Spirit to renew our minds and refresh our memories. The choice is up to us. Do we choose to respond to the Holy Spirit's gentle and quiet reminders, or do we forget and wander away?

The ministry message of Reasons for Hope* Jesus is anchored hope (Hebrews 6:19). The mission of Reasons for Hope*Jesus is to encourage believers to know what they believe and then to "rightly remember." "In the Upper Room" is a wonderful place to start.

Rightly remembering is an active, ongoing effort that requires our dedication and diligence. It is a work of the heart and the mind, not of the hands and the feet. It is less of something we "do" and more of something we "think." It involves partaking of core biblical truths to nourish our souls just as we partake of food to nourish our bodies. Jesus has told us that the hungry will always be fed: "Blessed are you who hunger now, For you shall be filled" (Luke 6:21)

The hunger Jesus spoke of is for Him: "Blessed are those who hunger and thirst for righteousness, For they shall be filled" (Matthew 5:6). A hunger for righteousness means that we must E-A-T of the Bread of Life to be filled.

E-A-T: An Acronym to Remember

This acronym "E-A-T" is meant to remind us of three important endeavors: Establish, Anchor, and Transform:

Establish our hearts with Christ's grace.

Hebrews 13:9 Be not carried about with divers and strange doctrines. For ***it is a good thing that the heart be established with grace..***

Anchor our soul with Christ's hope.

Hebrews 6:19 Which hope we have as an anchor of the ***soul****, both sure and steadfast...*

Transform our minds with the word of His Power.

Romans 12:2 ... be not conformed to this world: but ***be ye transformed by the renewing of your mind****, that ye may prove what is that good, and acceptable, and perfect, will of God.*

Hebrews 1:3 Who being the brightness of his glory, and the express image of his person, and ***upholding all things by the word of his power...***

We must always remember something that the disciples did not know as they sat at the table. . . we live because Jesus lives! Jesus has provided us with the true liberating freedom that only He can give. And He now sits at the right hand of the Father (Hebrews 1:3, 13, 8:1, 10:12, 12:2) and intercedes for us (Hebrews 7:25).

<*}}}><

MY Grace
IS sufficient
for you
2 CORINTHIANS 12:9

His Sufficient Grace

By Shari Abbott

May the mind of Christ live in me,
(1 Cor 2:16)
Every minute of every day.
May the grace that He has given me,
(2 Cor 12:9)
Establish my heart in His perfect way.
(Heb 13:9)

May I always reflect His wondrous love,
(2 Cor 8:24)
His sacrificial gift.
(Rom 5:8)
That others, in me, might also see,
His Light, His Joy, my Hope.
(1 John 2:8, Hab 3:18, 1 Cor 9:10)

May the hope that flows from only Him,
(Rom 15:13)
Anchor my soul, steadfast and strong.
(Heb 6:19)
So when the storms of life arise
He is my strength, my song.
(Ex 15:2)

In the face of all adversity,
In Him, I'll find my rest.
(Mat 11:28)
His promise is to comfort me,
(2 Cor 1:3-4)
In that, I know I'm blessed.

May my mind be ever transformed by Him,
(Rom 12:1-2)
Surrendered to His Word and will.
(1 Th 2:13, Mat 6:10)
For He's given me the Power I need,
(Heb 1:3)
His strength that does fulfill.
(2 Cor 12:9-10)

His Spirit now lives in me,
(Rom 8:9)
Assuring, I never am alone.
(Heb 13:5)
He's with me now, and forever will be,
(Mat 28:20)
My new and perfect home.
(1 Cor 3:16, Phil 3:20)

May I rest always in Jesus Christ,
(2 Cor 12:9)
the One and only Son.
(John 3:16)
Who's given me a redeeming love,
(Gal 4:4-5)
A grace that says, it's done.
(John 19:30)

I shall remember His will and ways,
(Deu 8:18, John 14:26, 2 Tim 2:8)
Sufficient grace He's given me.
(2 Cor 12:9, Eph 1:7)
I'll follow Him, all my days,
(1 Tim 6:11, 2 Tim 2:22, 1 Pet 2:21)
'Til my journey's end I see.
(2 Tim 4:6-7)

And then one day, to my delight,
I'll go to be with Him.
(2 Cor 5:8)
I'll see Him in His glory bright,
(Psa 24:10, 1 John 3:2, 1 Cor 13:12)
My Saviour, my reigning King.
(Luke 1:47, 1 Tim 1:17)

<*}}}><

Praise God

from whom all blessings flow

Praise Him

all creatures here below

Praise Him

above, ye heavenly host

Praise

Father, Son, and Holy Ghost

Amen.

Books & Resources from this Author

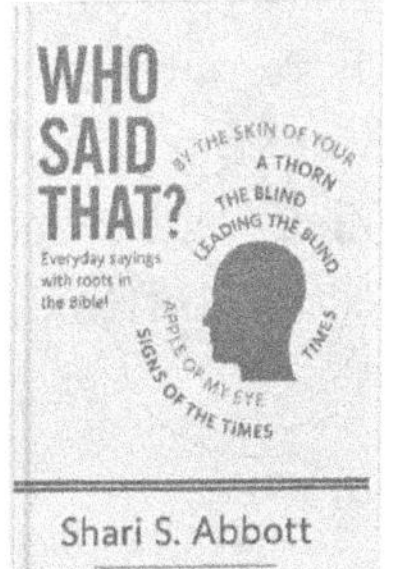

Who Said That? Common Everyday Sayings
This is a great book to give to unbelievers. It's simply a look at everyday sayings originating from God's Word. At the end of the book is a gospel presentation.

A Room with a View of Eternity—The Last Will & Testament of the Lord Jesus Christ

Take a seat at the Master's table. Learn about the Lord's final words to His faithful disciples (John 13-17), and the riches He gives to all who are His. This book will bless and encourage you, provide you with hope, and help you live in the joy of your salvation.

MISINTERPRETED 1&2— Misunderstood & Misapplied Bible Verses & Passages—Sometimes Scripture is wrongly taught with an intention to deceive, but most often it is unintentional. As Christians, we must be diligent in discerning truth —God's truth from His Word.

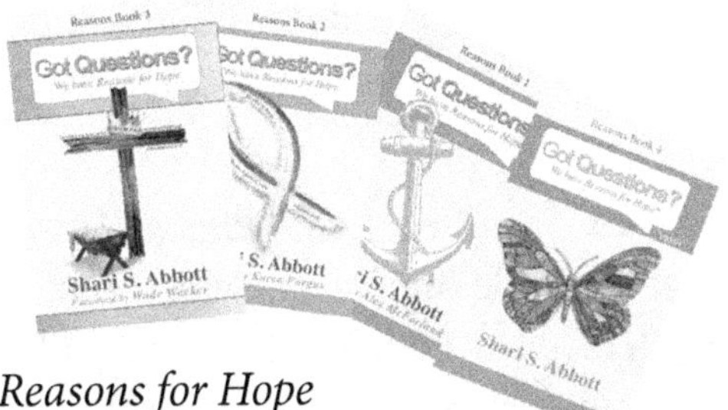

Got Questions? We have Reasons for Hope
Reasons Books 1, 2, 3 & 4

Real questions from real people. Each book has 30 questions and 30 answers with reasons for hope.

Why the Butterfly? Rightly Remembering Jesus—This book isn't about butterflies. . .it's all about Jesus! Discover how rightly remembering will establish your heart, anchor your soul, and transform your mind. A quick read that will give you a heavenly perspective on this journey we call life!

Remember Me - A Course About Rightly Remembering Seven video study sessions that teach rightly remembering and will ignite in you a desire to filter everything you think, say and do through the hope that is found in Jesus Christ. Learn how *rightly remembering* will establish your heart, anchor your soul, and transform your mind.

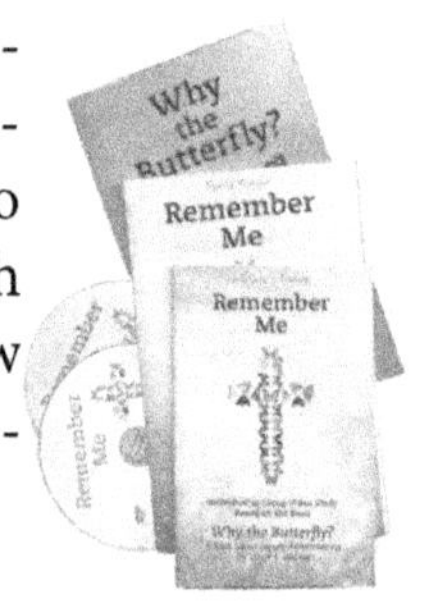

Fun with Shuns Learn the key doctrines of the Christian faith by understanding the many words in the Bible that end in "-tion". The study includes five short videos. If you can't fully explain why you believe what you believe, then you need this study. DVD and book for group or individual study.

Hear, See, Speak No Evil—Plus a Fourth Monkey The three little monkeys, with their proverbial quip, "Hear No Evil, See No Evil, and Speak No Evil," date back as far as 17th century. What biblical lessons do these monkeys offer? And what about the newest warning. . .post no evil?'

How to Witness to Jehovah's Witnesses, Apologetics Answers & Verses

Get prepared to defend what you believe and be able to present biblical truth the next time a Jehovah's Witness comes to your door. Don't be out-witnessed by a Jehovah's Witness. Free with the purchase of any Reasons Book(s). e Book available at Amazon.

Quotable Quotes - Words Worth Remembering is a treasury of timeless wisdom from Christian voices across the ages. Carefully chosen quotations are paired with Scripture references to encourage you to delve deeper into the biblical truths that relate to the insightful quotes—as a way to draw closer to the heart of God.

Forty Names of Jesus for Forty Days of Lent — A devotional book with short daily readings to inspire your mind and deepen your love for "The Risen Christ," your Shepherd, Savior, and King. When the forty days are complete, continue by exploring more names and titles of Jesus.

Rightly Dividing the Word of Truth —

With simple explanations and Scripture-centered teaching, this book will help you discover how a right understanding of Scripture brings clarity instead of confusion, confidence instead of doubt, and joy as you see how every part of the Bible fits together in God's perfect plan.

Seasons of Our Lives Daily Devotions

Each daily reading pairs a chosen Scripture with a warm, gospel-centered reflection, a probing question, and a heartfelt prayer, helping you see God's mercy, faithfulness, and love in every season of the soul.

Winter Snowflakes Daily Devotions:
December ~Light in the Long Night~
January ~Hope in the Waiting~
February ~Loved in the Cold~

Spring Blooms
Daily Devotions:
March ~Seeds of New Life~
April ~Rising with Christ~
May ~Growing in Grace~

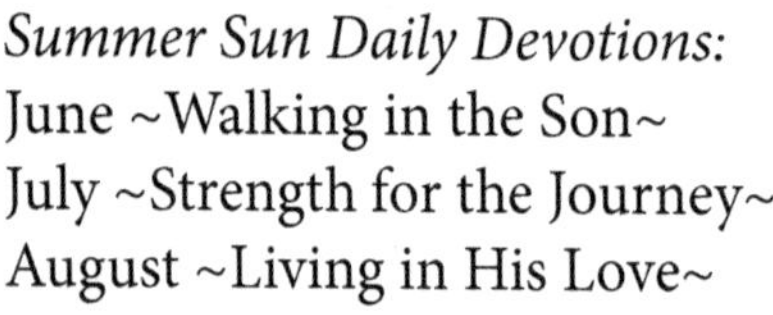

Summer Sun Daily Devotions:
June ~Walking in the Son~
July ~Strength for the Journey~
August ~Living in His Love~

Autumn Leaves Daily Devotions:
Septeber ~Lessons from the Harvest~
October ~Hearts of Gratitude~
November ~Eyes on Eternity~

This hope we have as an anchor for the soul, both sure and steadfast. (Hebrews 6:19)

Helping Christians to know Jesus better, by

Offering biblical answers and reasoning from God's Word, and

Promoting the benefits and joys of spending time with God in prayer and in reading and studying His Word, which leads to

Enjoying God, finding rest in Jesus, and living to honor Him and serve others.

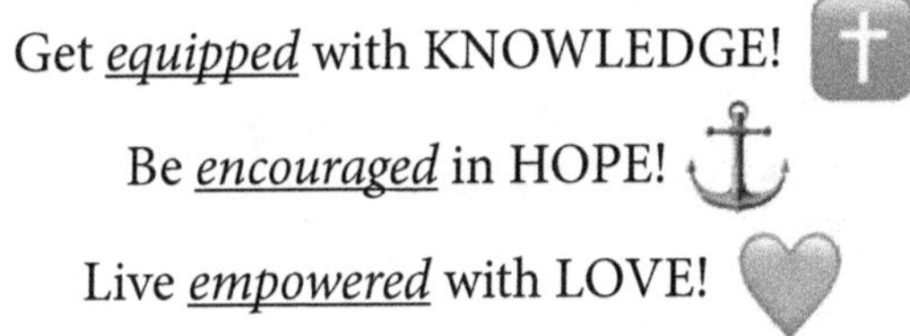

About Reasons for Hope* Jesus

Our ministry exists to glorify God by equipping Christians with biblical knowledge, understanding, and wisdom. By knowing and trusting God and growing in our understanding of His will and ways, we can change the world. Jesus is the reason this ministry exists, but YOU make it possible!

Visit www.reasonsforhopeJesus.com for biblical articles, instructional videos, and inspiring song videos.

Questions?

Email us at questions@reasonsforhopeJesus.com

Contact Us

Email us at hope@reasonsforhopeJesus.com

Connect With Us

www.reasonsforhopeJesus.com

Facebook: www.facebook.com/reasonsforhopeJesus/

Twitter: www.twitter.com/reasons4hope

YouTube: www.youtube.com/reasonsforhopeJesus

Visit the Store

www.reasonsforhopeJesus.com/store

Sign Up

At www.reasonsforhopeJesus.com for apologetics teachings and biblical encouragement with true hope and real joy.

May the God of hope fill you with all joy and peace in believing, that you may abound in hope by the power of the Holy Spirit. Romans 15:13

Have Hope!

Now hope does not disappoint, because the love of God has been poured out in our hearts by the Holy Spirit who was given to us.—Romans 5:5

Be Bold!

Therefore, since we have such hope, we use great boldness of speech.—2 Corinthians 3:12

[Praying] for me, that utterance may be given to me, that I may open my mouth boldly to make known the mystery of the gospel, for which I am an ambassador in chains; that in it I may speak boldly, as I ought to speak.—Ephesians 6:19-20

Share the Gospel

Since we have the same spirit of faith, according to what is written, "I believed and therefore I spoke," we also believe and therefore speak.—2 Corinthians 4:13

As it is written: "How beautiful are the feet of those who preach the gospel of peace, Who bring glad tidings of good things!"—Romans 10:15

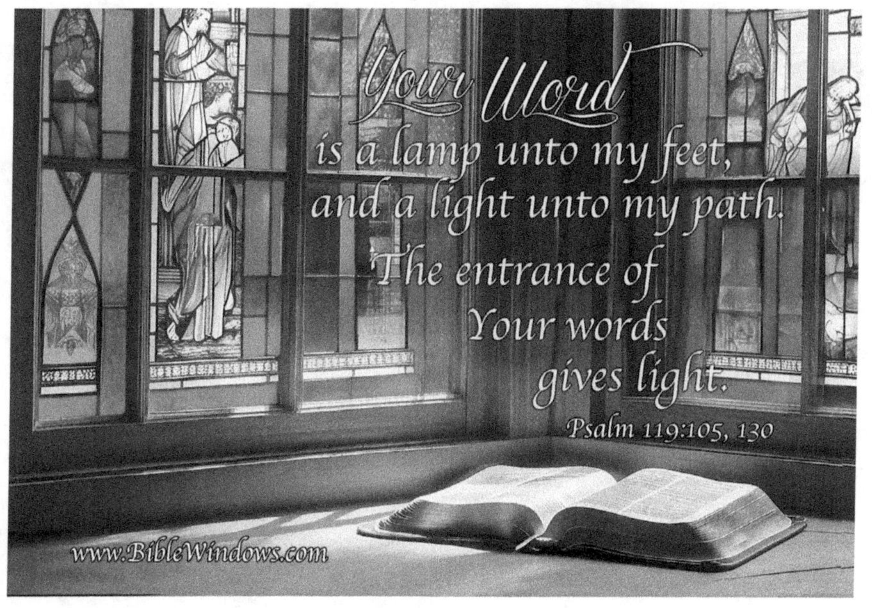

If Reasons for Hope*Jesus has blessed you, please consider supporting our ministry work. Your goodwill and generosity enable us to equip, encourage, and empower the body of Christ and reach the lost with the gospel of saving grace. www.reasonsforhopeJesus.com/donate

www.ingramcontent.com/pod-product-compliance
Lightning Source LLC
LaVergne TN
LVHW050643100826
845148LV00011B/1963

* 9 7 8 1 7 3 6 1 0 7 6 6 9 *